PRAYERSURGE

To Wendy,

Pray on!

A TRANSFORMING CALL, AN OVERCOMING LIFE

PRAYERSURGE

BILLIE CASH

Billie Cash

PS 4:5

AMBASSADOR INTERNATIONAL

GREENVILLE, SOUTH CAROLINA & BELFAST, NORTHERN IRELAND

PRAYERSURGE

A TRANSFORMING CALL, AN OVERCOMING LIFE

Cover design & page layout by A&E Media — Andrew Ramos

ISBN 1 932307 41 9

Published by the Ambassador Group

Ambassador Emerald International
427 Wade Hampton Blvd.
Greenville, SC 29609 USA
www. emeraldhouse.com

and

Ambassador Publications Ltd.
Providence House
Ardenlee Street
Belfast BT6 8QJ
Northern Ireland
www. ambassador-productions.com

The colophon is a trademark of Ambassador

DEDICATION

MY DEAR FRIEND, PEGGY

Her praying life has touched mine in friendship, love, sisterhood and ministry.

My prayers forever and forever shall be yours
William Shakespeare

AND TO THE MEMORY OF JAN LURTON AND DONNA WILKENING

These women had brief contagious lives of faith that breathed prayer.

What love has purposed, love shall carry through
Amy Carmichael

PRAY WITHOUT CEASING
I Thessalonians 5:17

ENDORSEMENTS

After having radiation therapy for an inoperable brain tumor in 2000, my 24/7 headache is gone…but Jesus is with me. I've always felt there was a reason for what has happened to me…I firmly believe I have been brought this far – to read your book and be challenged by it. I could not put it down. At first I was convicted…my prayer life had become stagnated…then I was encouraged. There is something I can do for others. I can pray. May the Lord bless and shine his light upon you always.

Penny Aplin
Fellow pilgrim on faith's journey
Bournemouth, England

Billie always writes from her soul but PRAYERSURGE is the very beating of her heart and her life walk with Jesus in prayer.

Nina Ruth Bruno
Young Business professional, sister in Christ
San Diego, California

Your writing style is so appealing to me and is giving me a boldness about the Lord… what He means to me…. You clearly made me see that we are called to pray with a discipline and a diligence. I am also learning that God is calling each of us…He is calling me to a new level of intimacy with Him. Thank you, Billie.

Bonnie Campbell
Navy wife extraordinaire, quilter, encourager, twenty year breast cancer survivor,
co-founder of Y-ME, National Capitol Area Breast Cancer Organization.
Springfield, Virginia

The overall view of your book is spiritual, calming, reassuring…. It's a prayer life builder – it helps to reset a more solid foundation, reassuring us of God's unconditional love… I pray that this book PRAYERSURGE be published in the millions, to be given or purchased by people all over the world so others may see the impact God's Love can have if they will give themselves to Him in faith and prayer. These words can stir the soul…change a nation. May each person who reads this book, in years to come, be blessed by the author and may she continue to be inspired to share the Holy Word of God.

Pat Russell
Intercessory Prayer Organizer for Director of Midwest Frontier Fellowship
Devoted volunteer at Midwest Palliative and Hospice Care center
Wilmette, Illinois

PRAYERSURGE is more than a surge; it's a TSUNAMI! The ministry of "one another" which Paul wrote about so often is "praying for one another." It percolates through every page. How lavishly God blesses the reader with His words through you, Billie. Bless the Lord, Oh my soul!

Wayve Berg Bradley
Bible teacher, mentor
Minneapolis, Minnesota

I have just finished PRAYERSURGE and all I want to do is pray…. writing prayers from God's Word…is a powerful way to pray…your book has stimulated me to "DO IT."

Jill White
Encourager, homemaker, Lover of God's Word
Poole,
Dorset, England

Billie so effectively communicated her passion for relationship with the Father through prayer that she ignited a spark in me as I read PRAYERSURGE. Read this book…begin an "electrically charged" relationship with the God of the universe through prayer. She helps you along with SURGING THOUGHTS and PRAYER FLOW at the end of each chapter. I really gained a new love for relational prayer.

Rachel Crabb
Speaker, golfer, author, The Personal Touch, Navpress
Prayer Consultant and National Director of Stonecroft Ministries
Wife of psychologist, author Dr. Larry Crabb
Denver, Colorado

I did not want the book to end. It is a mentor-piece for me. Billie has been obedient to God's Call to write what He has placed on her heart and is exemplifying in her life. A dear friend and mentor, she has encouraged me to surge in prayer. Prayer is a lifeline from God to help us endure the highs, middles and lows of life. Praise God for prayer. Experience…PRAYERSURGE in your life with God.

Stephanie R. Carbaugh
Wife, mother of Mia, professional organizer,
former lumber industry manager, daughter in faith
Lancaster, Pennsylvania

I have had the great privilege to worship, pray and fellowship with Billie and Roy regularly. When they pray, God's presence is in the room…by e-mail or in person. I am lifted to God…In my journey of almost 65 years on planet earth, I have met one person I felt qualified to write a book on prayer and that person is my sister in Christ, Billie Cash. I highly recommend this book to anyone who wants to grow with God.

Jules Dilday
Retired businessman, cowboy poet, beloved friend
Memphis, Tennessee

God expresses Himself through us. He calls us to pray for others. PRAYERSURGE will make you want to learn more about God's Holy Word and to pray, pray, pray. Thank God someone prayed for me. As I mature in my faith, I want to have a heart like Billie, caring, sharing, praying, loving and listening. You will not want to miss the blessing you will receive from this book.

Wendy Cogdill
Business owner, sister in Christ making a difference
Summerton, South Carolina

Looking out the window of my Vicksburg, Mississippi home, I watched the winds and rain of Hurricane Katrina's outer bands bend and break trees, wash holes and gullies in the back slope of my yard finally extinguishing electricity. I sought to get my mind off the storm by praying and reading Billie's latest book, PRAYERSURGE. As I read my emotions were calmed, my mind reassured, and my spirit lifted by the message and challenge of the book. Billie so many times "heard the call' to pray for me and my family – through my grand daughter Anna's rare genetic disorder. Billie's prayers were there – encouraging us, undergirding, interceding, reminding us of God's promises and they were answered with a successful liver transplant this year. She prayed me through the sudden death of my husband Dan, through my daughter's difficult and dangerous pregnancy and the birth of a premature son who was diagnosed with cerebral palsy, through hip surgery. Billie writes as she lives – in bursts of glorious energy. With her concise, almost poetic, style, she pulls us into this beautiful description of the work of prayer in a Christian's life. Her heart for God is revealed. Be careful as you read – this is a short book but the message is large – hear the call! Rise up in prayer! Love God! Love others! Be transformed! It is rich in real illustrations of prayer and in the real life direction of becoming a person of prayer…simple examples, simple sentences, simple lessons gleaned from God's Word validated in a lifetime of applying those lessons, woven together for our use as we learn to live…Billie lives a life of prayer, an overcoming life.

Phyllis Renfroe
Retired educator, compassionate grandmother, treasured friend
Vicksburg, Mississippi

Wow! In the midst of our own difficult transition into life in east Africa, God has spoken to us through Billie Cash's PRAYERSURGE. We have been reminded of truths we once knew and challenged to grasp truths we had not yet embraced. The Spirit of God Himself has surged within us both to pray and believe. To pray for God's promises to be accomplished in us, in others, and in this world, to believe that He will complete the good work He has begun.

Alan and Pam May
Missionaries ministering to orphans (13 at present)
Raising up a generation of godly children who will change the direction
of the AIDS-ridden, impoverished nation of Africa.
Eldoret, Kenya

Inspiring…practical. PRAYERSURGE ushers me into the holy place. Prayer needs to become more than it is in my life. God has pulled back the veil for me. This book has made me search deep within myself... Billie pursues the prayer life that Jesus had while on earth. It was His lifeline. It is hers. May it become mine.

Hope Roberts
Wife, mother of Faith and Grace, lover of the Word, daughter in faith.
Durham, North Carolina

Billie Cash's book, PRAYERSURGE, reminds readers of the importance, the power and the purpose of lifting our hearts to God in prayer. Drawing on the analogy of ocean waves surging onto the shore, Cash encourages readers in her story-like writing style to let our requests swell to God Almighty, the One who created us and loves us.

Christy Barritt,
Co-author of Changed: True Stories of Finding God in Christian Music
Chesapeake, Virginia

This book is challenging me to pray more, and also to look at prayer as an outflow of my heart's love for Jesus.

Mary Garborg
Avid reader
Prior Lake, Minnesota

Billie Cash's unique writing style breathes life into the key principles of prayer, which need to be learned by those who desire to pray with power. She unfolds her own journey to "powersurge" prayer, but also clearly and simply sets the pattern for readers who want to grow in skill using this powerful spiritual weapon. Billie tells of real prayer experiences revealing the struggle we encounter when we pray fervent, persistent, prayers resulting in God's amazing answers. The powerful chapter on brokenness should be read by every Christian for she emphasizes that real prayer must be motivated by love. When it is, we experience the Glory of God. The impact of a loving "prayersurge" group who comes together in belief and prays can affect the destiny of nations. All who read PRAYERSURGE will be challenged to give their lives to the magnificent ministry of prayer.

Lucille Sollenberger
Distinguished educator, BA, University of Nebraska,
MA University of Omaha, Doctoral studies at Stanford University
Miss Sollenberger possessed a wonderful ability to explain
"deep, complex, spiritual concepts in a way that every one could grasp."
Author of twenty two Bible studies for Stonecroft Ministries known as "Friendship
Bible Coffees" she also served as National Representative and Devotional Editor for
Progress magazine. Retiring in 1999, her work in the Word of God continues.

Billie takes us right to His throne of Grace with this book....

Ursula Bruno
Bible teacher, friend, prayer warrior
Poway, California

SCRIPTURE PAGE

"Who is this that rises...like rivers of surging waters?"
Jeremiah 46:7

"Know that the Lord has set apart the godly for Himself.
The Lord will hear when I call to him."
Psalm 4:3

ACKNOWLEDGEMENTS

Precious Praying friends, you have prayed me through. Your covering of faith and love breathed life, carrying me through the ebb and flow of this book.

Thank you Laura, Ann, Denise, Judy, Pat and Joyce for your faithfulness in prayer. You understand the mission of prayer.

The Calder Class is a loving family of brothers and sisters. Your gift of friendship and support is a treasure. You know my heart for prayer.

A special thank you to Peggy, Beth, Audrey, Peggy "in the cornfields", Hope and Stephanie to pray me through all I do. They all live in different states and are on call wherever I go, always responding.

My Internet friends are a wonderful praying group scattered through out the United States and England. They go into prayer when an alert comes forth. Thank you for being available.

A warm thanks to my husband Roy for his diligent hand in editing and to my publisher Samuel Lowry.

I have been moved to pray for others.
I have been inspired to meditate God's Word.
I have been challenged by the stories of praying lives.

God has met me once again.

I am humbled.

Thank you Lord, for allowing me to write and proclaim Your Love. Bless my friends and may they bring heaven to earth as they pray through the journey ahead. Thank YOU for praying friends.

Billie Cash

PRAYERSURGE

TABLE OF CONTENTS

"Who is this that rises....like rivers of surging waters?"
Jeremiah 46:7

FOREWORD

"Oh! For a closer walk with God," exclaimed William Cowper.

People who pray are seekers.
We long for God.
We look for Him.
We draw close to Him
On purpose in prayer.

In this book, I have looked back in time at voices of prayer that proved life could be lived by prayer alone.
Reflective lives
I have looked around at the world today, filled with anxiety, fueled by fatigue, fraught with danger.
Random lives
I have looked inside the Word of God for validation of men and women who knew how to live in possibility in the midst of ever present peril.
Revolutionary lives.

A praying life lives from the heart, a heart that has relationship with God.
A praying life knows the promises found in God's Word and prays them.
A praying life rises and flows in prayer for others altering their course by faith.
Redeemed lives

God is calling us to pray.
It is a transforming call to an overcoming life.
I am praying for you to answer.

Things learned on earth we shall practice in heaven

Robert Browning

Billie Cash WINTER 2005 • CORDOVA TENNESSEE

PREFACE

Prayer is communion
Communion is relationship
Relationship is belonging
Belonging is acceptance

Acceptance is birthed through love.
Love is the beginning of prayer
At first prayer is an idea we hear about but do not know
Experience urges us to try.
And so we do.
We are kicked, a whimper is heard,
We are wounded, a whisper is uttered,
We are silent outwardly but shouting inside
No words audible yet
But
Rising up within is prayer
Awkward at first, we cry out as newborn babies
God comes and claims us as His own.
Prayer is Love
Concern for others causes a quiet stirring within
Life challenges.
We begin to seek after God's answers.
He is present.
Are we?
Prayer is His Heart
Graciously, He arranges a moment of revelation
And then we comprehend the magnitude of a praying life.

It was an anticipated summer's day at the beach, a respite, and an escape
for me, I thought.
The sun at high noon was hotly blazing down while children scurried
around finding ways to enjoy it.
Buckets and spades in hand, they began to dig into the sand and armed
with boundless energy, they dumped it on each other, laughing and teasing.

I retreated under an umbrella, zapped by the heat.
After lunch, some of their noisy play ceased or blended with the sounds
of waves, effortlessly moving in sinc.
Settling in with a book, I finally drank in the ocean's activity, gazing
across the wide expanse of sky accented by streaks of azure and
tourmaline bleeding into a fiery opalescence against the horizon.
Such beauty...
A distant fishing trawler had dropped its lines while a Naval vessel was
headed out to sea.
A picture of going and coming
Suddenly the effect of listening to waves lapping languidly against the
shoreline seemed transportingly mesmerizing.
It was a pleasant sound, a solace, a dependable phenomenon.
There is ebb and flow to the tide every day.
It comes in and goes out.
Some days are gloriously clear.
Some are gray and etched with warning.
The tide is a surety.
So is the Love of God.
With spiritual awareness, I recognized within my heart what my mind
already knew.
What I glimpsed in the tide's movement was a personification of God's
Love for us.
Constancy
He beckons us to come.
We love God back through prayer
An insight, a work, a discipline, a joy, an empowering
He calls us to pray
Not a shy, quiet, introspective act, but a bold, sure, far reaching
acclamation emanating from intimacy found in community with a Living
God and given away,
Founded not on sinking sand but upon the certainty of His Word, a life
in the Spirit.
A consciousness dawned that day gathering momentum throughout the
waves of my faith journey
I would learn
To
SURGE IN PRAYER
Towards the shores of doubt and despair,
Toward illness and ignorance, possibility and promise,

Surge in belief and expectancy.
God's been writing this book upon my heart all of my life.

We overcome through prayer.

Pray your prayers through me, Lord.
Write your words upon my heart
Visit me with Your Presence.
Reveal Your Love for others through prayer.

Billie Cash WINTER 2005 • CORDOVA TENNESSEE

Chapter One

BELONGING TO GOD

It was a year of upheaval.
The United States mounted the biggest offensive of the Vietnam War, Beatles' music was the rage, and the mini-skirt hit the streets.

It was a year of firsts.
A woman by the name of Indira Ghandi became prime minister of India, the first Apollo test flight was a noted success, and a vaccine for Rubella was discovered.

It was a year of unrest.
The University of Texas was under siege from a gunman positioned on the top of the University Tower shooting at students arbitrarily like a hunter picks off game, Civil Rights activists were demonstrating in Canton, Mississippi and South African Prime minister Hendrik Verwoerd was assassinated.

It was a year of disasters.
The Arno River in Italy flooded Florence, a slagheap collapsed and engulfed the village school in Aberfan, Wales and Hurricane Inez assaulted the Lesser Antilles, making her way to Hispanola, Cuba and the Florida Keys.

The year was 1966.
Surging armies, medical breakthroughs, space achievements, nature's rebellion and turbulence in society,
Defining moments shaping a culture.
And God was redefining me.

I was present in Key West, Florida when Inez, a small but intense hurricane made landfall on Sept 21, 1966.

My husband Roy, a Navy fighter pilot was in the RAG (Replacement Air Group) for F-4 training. He had been a part of the air group that flew aircraft from the base inland when it was first predicted that Inez would hit the Florida tip where we were.

Roy returned when it seemed apparent that the hurricane had deviated and was now on a course headed due north churning up the Carolinas' coastline.

Inez fooled them.

During the night of the 20th she turned again and was headed south, straight for Key West.

Since Roy had been a part of the first wave of pilots flying aircraft away, he was allowed a reprieve, a day off, we thought.

Not so.

Awakening to the sounds of thunderous pelting rain, we turned the radio on and were told to prepare for a hurricane. The announcer was going over a "to do" list for the listeners; "do not put mail in mail boxes, do not send children to school, get water, food, batteries, flashlights, secure windows."

That directive was humorous for we were living in a basement efficiency apartment in the only octagonal stone house in Key West.

Built in the 1800's, it was unusual.

There were nooks, crannies, and multi-level floors surrounded by eight sided walls. The only windows we had were small openings of about 2 inches allowing in the tiniest ray of light. Our apartment was below street level.

It was like living in the bottom of a medieval mansion.

The house was included on the "Conch Tour," a tourist opportunity to see the town on a jitney open-air bus. People drove through our neighborhood weekly and peered quizzically at our odd shaped house. There were windows and porches upstairs but we had none to secure.

However, a storm *was* coming.

So, we had to get ready.

Our daughter Kellye was only 18 months old so I spent my days mothering. I knew what supplies I needed for her but we were counseled to bring all kinds of canned goods, powdered milk as well as water.

Locking up and battening down what we could, we headed for the Naval Base to spend the night in the enormous steel airplane hangar with hundreds of other families.

There was anxiety but also an intense energy in preparation.

People scurrying to get settled,

Cars lining up for parking in the hangar,

Supplies being counted, pooled,
Contingency plans for power outages,
Getting ready to wait.
There was a sense of safeguarded refuge in this substantial shelter.
And besides, Roy was with me.
Being with him always made me feel safe.

A large peripheral room with many windows was first chosen as the holding area for all the children but wisely changed as the evening progressed.
A theater in the interior, which had no windows, was the final choice for the night as all children with mothers in tow were instructed to go there.
The men worked throughout the night as wind and rain unleashed their relentless fury.
About midnight the eye of the storm had stalled over Key West.
Kellye had fallen asleep.
Roy found me and led me through the maze of people and gear outside the hangar into the eerie, black stillness of the ominous night.
It was as if we were momentarily in a vacuum with pending peril stalking.
There is mystery and danger surrounding a storm.
But there is also wonder for it is a combination of the elements of nature surging together in a mighty force.
Once I was back inside the hangar, I remember looking at Kellye and praying,
"Lord, You must know we are here, scared, trusting. Please take care of us."
That was about all I knew about prayer.
It was a call to God, mostly when you were in trouble.
I had faith in Him.
I knew I belonged to Him.
But my prayer was weak, uncertain, repetitious, child-like.
I hoped for the best.
It was to be a long night, no sleeping for me, just praying my simple prayer over and over, pleading to God.
I did not know what else to say.
Shortly after midnight, all the windows in the outer perimeter of the hangar blew out as screams and scuffling began to echo down the corridors and our men began an emergency response. The winds were clocked at 130 miles per hour, beating down heavily on Key West.
The waters begin to surge and so did my first attempt at prevailing prayer.
A storm surge is "simply water being pushed toward the shore by the force

of winds swirling around the storm. The slope of the continental shelf also determines the level of surge in a particular area. A shallow slope will allow a greater surge....." (1)

I knew nothing about a storm surge.

I knew less about surging prayer.

But God was training me.

This was my genesis.

Prayer prepares.

In 1900, a hurricane hit Galveston, Texas. There was no radar in those days and no advance preparation. Because it was a low lying area, the storm surge washed away homes, businesses and 6000 lives. Shallow slopes are easily taken out by surging water. The city fathers of this devastated city had the foresight to erect a sea wall, tall enough to protect Galveston from future hurricanes.

They were laying a foundation, groundwork for readiness.

And so must we.

We need radar and a wall.

Belonging to God is where you start.

Daylight did come to Key West.

The storm passed.

Blackened beaches with debris, trees downed, power lines gone, communication suspended but life sustained.

We had survived.

When you're hungry, pork and beans are not that bad for breakfast.

When you're anxious, hugging your child and husband is comfort.

When you cry out to God, He comes.

I knew He had heard my pitiful prayer.

He will hear yours.

An old hymn says it best:

Softly and Tenderly, Jesus is calling
Calling for you and for me
See on the portals He's waiting and watching,
Watching for you and for me
Come home,
Come home,
Ye, who are weary, come home.
Earnestly, tenderly Jesus is calling,

Calling, oh sinner, come home.

Coming home to Jesus is belonging and when we know we belong,
God creates a desire within us to pray.
Our relationship to God sets up a praying life that should be a natural as
breathing.

"My God, I pray better to You by breathing;
I pray better to You by walking than by talking" (2)

Belonging is the key.

Storms come.
We need to belong in a family of faith, brothers and sisters who will be
the wall.
Prayer is our radar.

Do you belong to God?
You can.

The Lord knows those who are his.... (3)

Let us begin to belong.
After all we need a family.

PRAYER FLOW

Lord,
It's just me,
Calling YOU.
I want to belong.
Would YOU come into my void?
I do not know how to live.
Somehow I know I need YOU.
Help me begin again.
I am child-like.
I will learn to walk and then run with YOU.
I do believe it is YOUR LOVE that makes it possible for me to belong.
Wash away the debris of my sin.

I've been in a storm most of my life.
Today, by faith YOUR LIGHT is breaking through.
Cleanse me.
Touch my soul.
Place YOUR LOVE into my heart through YOUR SPIRIT
I won't understand it all at first
But
Jesus, I come to YOU.
I believe.
Now I know I belong.

SURGING THOUGHTS

When did you know you belonged to God?

Did He use a storm?

Did you know that prayer brought you to God?

Everything that one turns in the direction of God is prayer
Saint Ignatius Loyola

Chapter Two

HEARING THE CALL

Why pray?

Compelled...
Alone...
Desperate...
Needy....

Comfort...
Courage...
Companionship....

Help, I cry!

YOU come.
YOU are here, always reaching to me, searching my heart, bringing fresh
expectation, lifting the weight, and asking to carry it.

I call.
YOU answer, Lord.

Yes, I am here, I always will be.
Beside you,
Beneath you,
Behind you, beloved child, bearing your burdens.
Give them to me.
Freed up, I will ask you to take up another's.
That is the work I give you.
When you call, I will hear and act.
I am listening.
I am changing you through prayer.
Once it was only about you,

Now it is for others.
Bring them to me in prayer
I will bring you through.
The world will become brighter
Because you prayed.

HEAR MY CALL

A praying life abides in relationship.
Belonging creates a thirst for intimacy, an appetite to know more about
God, quenched and satisfied only in His Word.
Why?
Because it is here we learn about God and build our relationship with
Him.
It is the next step.
His Word calls us to pray.
Jesus expects it.

And when you pray... (1)
But when you pray... (2)
This, then, is how you should pray... (3)
So, I say unto you: Ask... seek... knock. (4)
Then Jesus told his disciples...they should always pray. (5)

Trust must begin.
Truth is found in God's Word.
In it we can hear God calling us.
Opening the Word of God, I can ask God to speak to me.
He will.
Today this is what I heard.
The story of Hannah in I Samuel reached for my hand.
It is the remarkable story of a woman's steadfast, belief in prayer.
In spite of the daily rivalry of another wife, Peninnah, for the affection of
their shared husband Elkanah, Hannah persisted in her call to God.
Talk about strife in a family,
Two wives,
One husband.
Peninnah had children.
Hannah was barren.
There was a husband, who loved her enough to give her a double portion

of meat,
An adversary who provoked and aggravated her so much she could not eat.
Hannah wept, languished and sobbed out her plea to God for a son.
How long had this been anguish?
The Bible tells us *year after year this man* (Elkanah) *went up from his town to worship and sacrifice*... (6)
So year after year he took his wives to the temple and Hannah coped with the ridicule, harassment of Peninnah.
How many years had she endured?
Many.
Jealousy is not new.
Dysfunction has darkened centuries.
Hearts get broken.
From God's Word, we see a vigilant pertinacious woman who believes He will answer. Going into the temple, she not only lays down her lament once again, her grieving childlessness, this time she declares with intention a vow.
It is a mother's entreaty, a negotiation.
Hannah strikes a bargain with God.

O Lord Almighty, if you will only look upon your servant's misery and remember me, and not forget your servant but give her son, then I will give him to the Lord for all the days of his life.... (7)

What does she say?

Hannah addresses her prayer to the LORD ALMIGHTY
Identifies herself as being his servant,
Lays bare her heart's misery,
Asks to be remembered.
Amazingly, she not only asks to conceive.
She asks for a son, promising to give him back to the Lord.
Pouring out her soul unto her God, Hannah's lips began to move but her voice was not heard.

Hannah was praying in her heart. (8)

Eli, the priest, was watching intently and misinterpreted her impassioned state.
He thought she had been drinking wine and was out of control.

She explained, *Not so, my lord…I am a women deeply troubled…I have not been drinking wine… I have been pouring out my soul to the Lord. Do not take your servant for a wicked woman; I have been praying out of my great anguish and grief.* (9)

Hearing her explanation, Eli pronounced blessing upon her.

… May the God of Israel grant you what you have asked of him… (10)

She left with release and hope.
Hannah and Elkanah then worshipped before the Lord, traveling home together and there she did conceive. In time, a son was born, named Samuel, *because I asked the Lord for him.* (11)

A lot still remained to be done in the rearing of Samuel.
Remembering the annual sacrifice to the Lord as well as her promise to fulfill her vow, Hannah had much to accomplish. Staying at home to nurse and wean him, she prepared to return with a proper sacrifice to the temple, ceremonially giving him over to be trained for the service of the Lord in the care of the high priest Eli,
A woman keeping her word.
Her prayer, recorded in the second chapter is filled with adoration, awe, and allegiance to the Sovereign Lord.
One cannot read it without looking inside one's own heart.
Phrases capture a corner, an empty space within you.

My heart rejoices in the Lord; In the Lord, my horn is lifted up…. There is no one holy like the Lord…No Rock like our God…for the Lord is a God who knows…he humbles and he exalts…he lifts the needy from the ash heap…For the foundations of the earth are the Lord's…He will guard the feet of his saints…It is not by strength that one prevails; those who oppose the Lord will be shattered. He will judge the ends of the earth…He will give strength to the horn of his anointed…. (12)

Samuel grew up in the temple and became a prophet of great stature.
As Eli grew old and his sons grew wicked, Samuel flourished in godliness as a true servant, ministering under Eli's authority.
One night while lying in bed, Samuel heard his name being called out.
He thought it was Eli but it was God.

Confused, he went to Eli and was assured that it was God, indeed and then he was told how to respond.

Samuel said, *Speak, for your servant is listening.* (13)

Judgment was coming now to the children of Israel.
God would require Samuel to be a voice of Truth, a loyal man of God.

...The Lord revealed Himself to Samuel through his word.
And Samuel's word came to all Israel. (14)

What did I learn from this story?
Did I hear from God?
I did.
Did you?
I saw a portrait revealed of an ardent woman yearning to be a mother, trusting in a God who could do the impossible, a woman bold enough to ask for it.
God honored her faith.
I heard from a woman who knew how to thank God and to embrace prayer as an offering in such a way that today her prayer became mine as I read it.
I understood that the gift she was given had to be surrendered to God.
She gave back;
She was grateful.
She recognized her Giver.
I absorbed the life of a devoted young man, a servant highly privileged to hear his name called out by the God he served.
A nation was changed because of Samuel's life.
Today, mine was also.
I read all of this in the Word of God.
When I finished reading, I sensed Him calling me through the impressions gleaned from this story.
I discovered I move closer to God through His Word.
So can you.
If I purpose to receive it into my life, it will eventually take hold of my heart and become the foundation of a praying life.
Prayer can become the fruit of the Word.

"So the Word of Christ resides in our heart, in all its richness...in it we are rooted, on it we are founded, by it we order our conduct in life, and all the time we overflow with praise and thanksgiving...." (15)

A heart trained to trust finds a voice in prayer, surging for others.

What a friend we have in Jesus, all our sins and griefs to bear.
What a privilege to carry everything to God in prayer.
Are we weak and heavy laden, cumbered with a load of care?
Precious Savior, still our refuge, Take it to the Lord in Prayer.

God's Word stirred within me the impetus to pray.

"Whatever happens...I must continue to believe in a glad outcome – but I must also prepare for whatever else may lie ahead." (16)

Prepared to pray through.
Prayer is a work God's calls us to do.
Is He calling you?

PRAYER FLOW

Almighty God,
I see that prayer is a work of the heart, a work of faith.
It becomes a Divine equipping, opening the way for the dreams of others.
YOU have given me YOUR WORD.
I need its characters, their stories and their marked faith as a picture of how YOU have answered prayer through the ages.
Nothing just happens.
YOU originate and participate.
How comforting that YOU can take a frail utterance that is barely audible born from a crushed heart and it becomes a surge of confident expectation erasing doubt.
I want to pray with assurance and I long to develop confidence to do so by reading YOUR WORD
So call me, Lord, every day.
YOU know where I am.
Because of Jesus' Name, I will hear and respond.

SURGING THOUGHTS

Have you ever taken a story from the Bible, reading reflectively and internalizing its impact?

Have you ever entered into a time of prayer based on what you learned?

Would journaling your thoughts about the passage help your praying life to emerge?

Does God still call to us through His Word?

> **The door of prayer has been open**
> **Ever since God made man in his own image.**
>
> George MacDonald

A CLEAR DEVOTION

For out of Love exhales a living light
A light that speaks – a light whose breath is prayer

H. Coleridge

Chapter Three

RISING TO PRAY

Prayer is learned.

"There is a sense in which prayer needs to be taught to a child of God no more than a baby needs to be taught to cry. But crying for basic needs is minimal communication, and we must soon grow beyond that infancy. The Bible says we must pray for the Glory of God, in his will, in faith, in the name of Jesus, with persistence, and more. A child of God gradually learns to pray like this in the same way that a growing child learns to talk."(1)

Relationship to God through Jesus establishes our connection to Him.
We belong.
We open the Word of God.
He calls us to pray.
At this point we sense we are to know more, to become more.
What happens is the dawning that the *"more"* involves a process we have long attempted to escape – discipline.
All the influential saints of God have had to embrace this word.
Many of them knew there would be training ahead.
Today we have their simulating stories to encourage us to be more for God.
George Mueller was such a man.
He *practiced* prayer by praying.
Operating an orphanage in Bristol, England, he cared for as many as two thousand orphans at a time. Mr. Mueller was also involved in missions throughout the world. For two thirds of the last century, this man prayed in the funds needed to sustain the orphanage.
Millions of dollars came in as he prayed.
Known as one of the most effective men of prayer in his day, people wondered what his *secret* in prayer was.
"In the spring of 1841, he made a discovery...regarding the relationship between meditation and prayer that transformed his spiritual life.... He said, 'The first thing I did after having asked a few words of blessing upon

His precious word, was to begin to *meditate* on the Word of God...for the sake of obtaining food for my own soul...the object of my meditation. The result...there is always...confession, thanksgiving, supplication or intercession mingled with my meditation and... my inner man almost invariably is...nourished and strengthened. I dwell on this...because of the immense spiritual profit and refreshment I am conscious of having derived from it myself.... By the blessing of God, I ascribe to this mode the help and strength which I have had from God to pass in peace through deeper trials, in various ways...having now above fourteen years tried it this way, I can most fully...recommend it.'" (2)

So George Mueller discovered that if he meditated on scripture, the act of turning over in his head and heart the words of the Bible, digesting them for his own life, something happened to his soul.

It was renewed.

Prayer began to rise as he cleansed his own heart, thanking God.

He then prayed for others.

Webster's dictionary tells us that supplication is a "humble request, prayer, petition" and intercession is the "act of interceding, mediation, pleading in prayer in behalf of another or others."

Prayer rising for others.

Food, clothing shelter, heat, staff requirements, rent must have been a part of the supplication born from his heart, a cleansed heart made ready to pray,

Intercession for boys and girls with personalities, dreams, childhood illnesses, behavioral quirks, spiritual maturity, hopes.

George Mueller learned to lay down his life in prayer and take up the Word of God daily as His own prayer.

Meditating on the Word of God moved God's heart for his children.

A plan to pray, a way to pray, a practice of praying.

The habit learned was a spiritual discipline that brought liberty and vitality to life.

Prayer is a miraculous work

It still is.

Habits are learned.

Practice produces.

We learn by practice.

God knows we will be changed by what we practice.

Prayer changes us first.

Seeking HIM in His Word, reminds us of who we are because of Who He is.

O Lord, you have searched me and you know me.
You know when I sit and when I rise;
You perceive my thoughts from afar
You discern my going out and my lying down;
You are familiar with all my ways
Before a word is on my tongue
You know it completely, O Lord. (3)

Reading, thinking and absorbing these words cause a deep wellspring of joy and gratitude to rise up within my soul, for they reveal that our God does know us.
We are not numbers or mistakes.
God is the very Creator of our lives.

You hem me in – behind and before
You have laid your hand upon me. (4)

He disciplines us in godliness through habits and sometimes we are hemmed in – for our own good.
He knows what each day will bring for HE is ahead orchestrating our way.

You knit me together in my mother's womb. (5)

He knew the instant we were created.
Does anyone else have that kind of knowledge?

How precious to me are your thoughts O God!
How vast is the sum of them...they outnumber the grains of sand,
When I am awake, I am still with you. (6)

He thinks about us all day and all night.
Is there any attention given that encapsulates us every moment?

Search me, O God and know my heart,
Test me and know my thoughts.
See if there be any offensive way in me
And lead me in the way everlasting. (7)

We do have offensive ways.
We need to be led in the everlasting way, which is HIS.

My Bible is my friend.
I got serious about reading it in 1969.
My husband gave me a Bible on our sixth wedding anniversary. It was small and white, a little larger than a bride's Bible so to me it was a romantic gesture.
I loved the gift of it, but I placed it on a shelf.
I knew where it was, but it did not get picked up very often.
As life began to unfold for me, I would occasionally leaf through the pages, always finding my way to the Psalms.
I enjoyed poetry and literature in college and the poignancy of the Psalms drew me.
David's highs were high and his lows were low and I identified with the ebb and flow of his life because it was real life.
Roy went out sea and he came home and in between, I had to learn how to live, to flow.
He did that for thirty years.
One day I knew I was to learn *more* by reading that dear little book and in it I found a home for my wavering heart.
Restless I was.
Resolved I became; to live in it, know it, commit it to memory.
Refreshed I grew into loving the Word of God
It worked.
I had time.
Time to learn to pray and live in the Word.
It seems that we tend to postpone living until the right circumstances come along.
Daydreams that begin with *"when we, if we could, but maybe when"* set us up to prepare to live in the future,
We must live in the present.
God never misses one of our days.
Deployments, long absences away from home for the service man, claimed Roy from us for months at a time.
This lifestyle was to become a way of life.
How could I live inside it?
I would fantasize faraway places, looking at travel magazines, praying, dreaming, scrimping, saving, hoping to be able to go and see him sometime

in a foreign port.

Such complete excitement and anticipation of meeting the ship, welcoming him on a pier, seeing his face would be a movie moment.

Some precious time together as a couple would make the long separations in between *almost* worth it.

I said, *almost*.

In 1972, we rendezvoused in Hong Kong. It was a scheduled port, an R/R (rest and recreation) for our men, a time "off the line" away from danger.

They were in a war.

I was at home raising children.

We were both doing our jobs.

The war was Vietnam.

This was to be our brief intermission from the consuming pressures we lived with daily.

How thrilled I was!

I had never flown so far, about ten thousand miles.

Nervous, a little scared and anxious but eager I was to go.

My mother, Frances, and my grandmother, known as Mama Ofe, came to San Diego to take care of our two children, a rowdy little son named Carey, age 2 and a quiet, shy daughter Kellye, age 7. I know it is hard for some people to believe that Kellye was as I have described but at that time she was an introvert like her father.

I knew they would have the best care with Nana and Mama Ofe, so when I boarded the plane with all my heart I praised God for His provision.

I had peace.

He had made a way for me to go when there seemed to be none.

My little beloved book went with me.

By then I was becoming familiar with it and the scriptures memorized from my youth were now rising up within me during my prayer times.

I wanted to become a woman of prayer.

I desired to substantiate my life with Truth.

There is no new Truth.

Truth comes from God's Word.

I was learning to pray the Word of God for myself and for my family.

I did not realize it then but God was coaching my heart, preparing it to intercede for others.

When I arrived in this exotic port, halfway around the world, my joy spilled over in waves of thanksgiving. I tucked away every second we spent together into my heart's memory, knowing I would pull them out and relive each one when it was time to return home.

We had ten days of beloved, intimate togetherness, laughing and loving, sightseeing and shopping and all to soon they were over and it was time for me to go.

The day my plane took off, there were tearful goodbyes as almost 200 Navy wives boarded planes knowing they were going back to responsibility as the men headed back to war.

I shall never forget the weeping sound that I heard and the anguished looks reflected in the women's faces as they said their last goodbyes, dreading going home alone. Finding my seat, out came my dear little book – God's Word and I opened it. Seconds after so doing, a young Navy wife newly married came over to me. She was crying uncontrollably. Seeing the Bible open on my lap must have encouraged her to come to me for touching my shoulder she asked me to pray for her.

Right there, kneeling down beside me on this 747 airplane that was loaded with emotionally charged Navy wives and many other passengers, prayer began to rise for I knew my Heavenly Father was present guiding me into prayer for another.

As I began to pray for this tender one who desperately needed the promises found in God's Word, my own heaviness was lifted.

What confidence He gives in such times.

We hugged and she returned to her seat and I returned to my own reverie.

It was a long flight of many hours to San Diego.

My precious little book comforted me as tears spilled down my cheeks many times and ran onto its pages, staining them forever as I worshipped and wept my way home through the waves of doubt and fear threatening to sweep away my faith.

Memories flooded.

The portrait an artist had painted of us in shades of garish gold and muddy brown, odd coloring but uniquely us,

The classical ensemble of musicians that always played "Laura's Theme" when we walked into the hotel dining room, smiling at us with a twinkle in their eyes,

The visit to the pearl shop,

An exceptional Chinese dinner aboard a floating restaurant,

The intent faces of the boat children who dove into the waters trying to retrieve coins,

The story of the Chinese man who had a home with four levels and a wife for each one representing summer, fall, winter and spring.

Memories matter.

But deep inside, surging prayer was gathering velocity.

Meditating God's Word had deepened my faith and solidified my trust in prayer.

I was learning and remembering in gratitude.

Memories reinforce.

Habits were beginning to emerge.

Choice, to pray or not to pray.

Understanding what God requires.

Confession cleanses.

I needed to be made clean.

I bathed my body daily.

My soul needed bathing as well.

God is holy.

Sin shuts down prayer.

Meditating the Word of God causes prayer to rise.

Flowing with instruction, promise and illustration, the Bible sets us up to surge in prayer for others.

Thought, habit, lifestyle come together forming the sweet discipline of a praying life.

George Mueller learned to pray with power because he met God in His Word.

He *practiced*.

Interceding for others was his life's work.

I wanted to pray for others.

I learned by practicing.

So can you.

Holy Spirit, breathe on me, until my heart is clean. ✳
Let sunshine fill its inmost part without a cloud between.
Breathe on me, Breathe on me,
Holy Spirit, breathe on me.
Take thou my heart, cleanse every part.
Holy Spirit, breathe on me.

Holy Spirit, breathe on me
My stubborn will subdue.
Teach me in words of living flame what Christ would have me do.
Breathe on me, Breathe on me,
Holy Spirit, breathe on me.
Take Thou my heart, cleanse every part.
Holy Spirit, breathe on me.

A clean heart rises in prayer.

Pray for one another (8)

How long are we do this work?
Part of the inscription from Roy in my treasured little book says it best,
"...for as long as the Bible lasts."

Forever.

PRAYER FLOW

O Lord of the scripture,
Indeed YOU know me.
Searching my heart, you have shown me my sin, my loneliness, my anger,
my disappointment, my regret.
So I lay them down before YOU for they are obstacles to wholeness.
Cleanse me, Lord.
Wherever I am, YOU are there.
Sitting, rising, going out, lying down,
Even as my words to YOU are formed, YOU know them before I speak them!
Such knowledge overwhelms me with gratitude.
I cannot flee from YOU.
I cannot hide.
I cannot dwell in any height or depth unknown by YOU.
I will praise YOU for YOUR WORD tells me that I am fearfully and
wonderfully made.
In the secret place YOU knew me.
All the days ordained for me were written in YOUR BOOK, which is now
my book
Meditating upon its words brings assurance and my faith surges in belief.
Thank YOU for thinking about my life every day.
Take care of the wicked, Lord.
Give me YOUR HEART for others.
Nurture discipline in me.
Teach me to pray.
Make ready a praying life of intercession.
O Lord, I want others to know that what YOU have done for me, YOU

will do for them.
Intervene, intercept them.
Keep me faithful.
I will rise to pray.
It is Your Will.
Lead me on, Thou Great Jehovah
In Jesus' Mighty Name, I pray.

SURGING THOUGHTS

How can I pray with confidence?

Can I learn to meditate upon God's Word?

Will discipline bring liberty?

The whole meaning of prayer is that we may know God
Oswald Chambers

Chapter Four

LOVING GOD MORE

Prayer is Love.

> The worth and excellency of a soul
> Is to be measured by the object of its love.
> Henry Scougal

Love, that's it.
Do we love God *more*?
What do we love?
Our comfort, our way, our gifts, our appetites, our achievements, our possessions, our world and all that we are.
We love ourselves.
But do these *loves* fulfill our deepest yearning to be loved?
They do not.
What does then?

...With this in mind I kneel in prayer to the Father from whom every family in heaven and earth takes its name, that out of the treasures of his glory he may grant strength and power through his Spirit in your inner being that through faith Christ may dwell in your hearts through love. (1)

This kind of Love comes from God, through the indwelling Jesus.
I hear the call to pray because I am His.
I rise to pray and seek Him in His Word and then I begin to focus on what He says in the Word.
Before I know it I am praying the Word and it becomes my word.
My heart wells up in love for the author of the Word so I begin to know who He is and I.
I begin to Love Him supremely.
Loving Him *more* expands my view of this world.
It must include others.

I must create space for Him,
Soul space so that my love can grow.
He calls us to search and find Him.

Come near to God and He will come near to you. (2).

My heart is the training ground for loving God.
I must Love Him enough to be present to Him in relationship daily,
moment to moment.
"…Instead we opt for the emotional crutch of pursuing spiritual activity as
a substitute for the emotionally vulnerable and time consuming option of
pursuing a Person." (3)
Loving God is a sweet vocation.

God watches over the way of the righteous. (4)

He watches to see how much we love.
Many people respect God but have not yet begun to love Him.
When I choose to spend time with someone special I prepare, plan and
participate.
I show up.
I want my love to be revealed by my actions.
I want it to be visible.

God loves to be loved.

Let us be self controlled, putting on faith and love as a breastplate. (5)

So I must choose to love Him, to put on His Love.
Our Heavenly Father reached down to us and sent Jesus because of Love.
We must reach out for Jesus daily and ask for more love.
But our stuff gets in the way.

Prayer is love, loving God back.
What you love will characterize your life.

Catherine the Great, whose life was filled with a search for earthly love, treasures,
lovers and acceptance, wrote in her own epitaph, "Catherine loved art."
Alexander the Great loved the pursuit of power and at the end of his life
he was saddened that there were no more lands to conquer.

What do you love?

Be forewarned.

God will examine your love.

In one of our many moves as a Navy family, we lost a life's savings on a home in southern California during our daughter Kellye's senior year in high school.

It was devastating.

Talking to my mother on the phone, I began to sob.

I felt a keen accountability, being the one left in charge of selling the home.

I remember sending my husband the telegram about the loss.

He replied, "It's only money. We are rich in other things. Press on."

And so we did.

Examinations are good for us for they reveal what we really know about God and ourselves.

They uncover false loves.

We discover what we love.

God shows us how to live from the heart.

His is a consuming Love, purifying, exposing what is hidden.

He loves people.

Loving them is loving Him.

Praying for others is loving God back.

His name was Goldie and he was a cab driver on the island of Jamaica.

We were fortunate to be able be there a few days to unwind and escape winter's demands.

Early that morning in my waking prayer I was thanking God for allowing us to come on this trip and asking Him to prepare our day, our opportunities, our hearts.

"Lord if there is any one YOU want us to intercept with YOUR LOVE, make it obvious."

He did.

As we begin to ride across the island we began to talk with Goldie.

He was father to several children but made sure we knew he had never married.

His English skills were excellent.

Troubled about the economy, the storms, the uncertainty, his conversation was mostly about hardships in this island country. As we arrived at our destination and said goodbye, I was stirred to leave something with him that would point the way to God.

I remembered I had some scripture cards in my purse so I pulled one out and gave it to him. Then I felt prompted to say, "God loves you Goldie, seek Him for He knows who you are and loves you."

An expression of intrigue and possibility brought forth a slow smile that widened across his deeply tanned countenance weathered with living.

He thanked me profusely for the card, even bowing a bit as if my speaking about God to him was a longed for happening.

He assured me he would keep the card.

I prayed many times that he would find his way to the Love of Jesus.

God's love prompts us to pray and then act.

In Jamaica, beautiful, pristine beaches of purest white sand beckon the weary traveler, broken by empty choices, exhaustion or used up lives to come, sit down a spell and enjoy a break.

Sand between your toes on a warm tropical day feels good.

Sand in your bathing suit does not.

But pearls come from creatures that live in the sand.

In fact, the first grain creates irritation in the oyster's shell until the oyster begins the process of building up a defense, emitting a bodily substance, which begins to harden, encapsulating the single grain of sand. It is an effort to combat the intrusion and after a period of time, something very beautiful evolves from a grain of sand, a pearl.

Life exposes what we love.

God takes our circumstances and loves us through them, changing what we began with and creating something *more*.

So we must unmask our hearts and internalize some questions.

Do we love enough to believe He is in the process we are in presently?

Do we love Him enough to allow Him to create something beautiful?

Do we love Him enough?

"Pearl living" is not "grain of sand" living.

Today I opened His Word and asked for His Love.

Here is what I heard: *The Lord is near* (at *hand*) (6)

A loving God is always near to us.

His Word shows us stories of people's lives and we can see ourselves in them.

Peter 's life was given to us as a pearl.

Robust Peter would probably have laughed out loud at such a statement.

Here's why I view his life as a pearl in the making

When Peter the disciple got out of the boat in tormented seas to come to the Lord, to walk across the water, his eyes were riveted upon the Master.
The others thought the Lord was a ghost.
Peter knew the Lord was near.
He was drawn to attempt something he had never done before – to walk on water.
Why?
Because the Lord asked him to *come*.
Suddenly realizing his circumstance, what he was attempting to do, he became afraid.
Fear comes too.
I can picture Peter grasping, struggling for the hand of Jesus.

Immediately Jesus reached out his hand and caught him 'You of little faith…why did you doubt?'…and the wind died down. (7)

The overwhelming fear did also.
I love Peter.
The sinking, doubting, fickle, faithless follower of Jesus.

You are not one of those disciples, are you? I am not. (8)

Just like us.
Peter loved His Lord and so he reached out for help because the Lord was near.
Loving God doesn't mean we won't let Him down.
We are weak.
It means He will always reach for our hand.
That's the Love that will never let go of your life.
I learned this truth in a fresh way in 1998 when I went to England to record my CD of worship music.
Fear was crouching, waiting for me.
Failure began to drape itself across my soul, encumbering me, dragging me down.
In waking hours, waves of anxiety and inadequacy came relentlessly and I found myself with a cloud cover masking the presence of God, trying to obliterate His love.
It was dark and foreboding, an oppressive threatening heaviness settling in on me.
Cold perspiration beads popped up all over my body as I walked the floor

and wondered out loud why I had come to do this project.

A plateau of prayer unknown by me was being raised up.

To get there I was to bow down.

I fell to my knees, crying out.

Bowing down did something for my soul

I was humbled, subjected to true Loving Authority.

I had never kneeled to pray.

It had never occurred to me to do so.

Bowing was an outward demonstration of allegiance, of my unashamed, dependent love for the only One who could equip me, rescue my fainting heart, cause me to take the leap or the first tiny step toward possibility.

God met me.

The act of kneeling was a submission to my King.

I discovered that as soon as I prayed on my knees, I could stand in belief.

I proclaimed out loud my position in Christ Jesus.

"I know who I am. I am God's child, my peace was bought by the Blood of the Lamb."

Seizing the offense, as a football player would do, I then declared some of the promises that are mine because of His love.

They are found in His Word and they are ours for the praying.

Trembling but now steady I was ready to proceed with the task ahead.

Something significant happened to my faith journey that day.

I turned a corner in prayer.

My faith in God's Love had walked across the waves of worry and false warnings and found security in the hand of my God who was near.

I recorded the album.

It was God's music and it flowed with His message.

He blessed.

He knew I would sink.

He was on watch.

I wasn't to walk across the water as Peter did.

I was to kneel in prayer.

He is always keeping vigil over life.

I had to learn to kneel.

He did not require it but by bringing me to my knees, the forces of darkness *saw* that I bow to the King of Kings.

Oh, how oppression runs when we bow down.

It is an act of love.

We can feel abandoned, but we are not.

We get caught off guard but God does not.

"One must face the fact that all the talk about His love for men...is not mere propaganda but appalling truth." (9)

Kneeling is a manifestation to the unseen world of our love and I have begun my day every day since January 1998, on my knees.

Start there and a disposition to pray will be carried in your life, sweeping you from disquiet restlessness to a sure and imminent resolution.

We have prayer work.

We are called to pray for others.

Loving God is kneeling before circumstance so that we may stand in strength, His.

Understand that the waves will attempt to wear down our souls.

But the Lord is near, superintending and alert.

He takes our hand, we bow, and then we rise in faith because of love.

Prayer begins to surge, enveloping the winds of change, swells of uncertainty, establishing trust.

We can intercede for others because He is interceding for us.

Prayer goes forth like ripples on a pond, rushing currents in a river or crashing breakers billowing across an ocean delving down deeply into the places of depravation.

The prayer waves of intercession crest and swell, loop, pulsate and deliver the love of God. Over and over, saints through out the ages have experienced this work of wonder,

God intercepting others through praying people.

It is indeed a sweet discipline.

Peter had a work to accomplish.

Remember all the promises he had made?

They were words of good intention.

He did not keep them – in the beginning.

He failed.

"Peter failed but I think there were eleven bigger failures sitting in the boat." (10)

And so will we.

But the One who called us to Himself, Jesus,

The One who calls us to pray,

The One who speaks to us from His Word,

This One who loves us *will not fail*.

Hardship will come.

*Endure hardship as discipline... strengthen your feeble arms and weak knees...
make level paths for your feet...* (11)

I will always love Peter
At least he got out of the boat.
"It was Peter's willingness to risk failure that helped him to grow." (12)
And so must we.

Our God asks us the same question that he asked Peter, *Simon, son of John,
do you truly love me more than these?* (13)

Praying for others is loving God *more*.
He is the supply for *more* love.
The Hymn writers knew we would need messages about God 's Love.

*I was sinking deep in sin far from the peaceful shore
Very deeply stained within, sinking to rise no more
But the Master of the sea heard my despairing cry
From the waters lifted me, now safe am I.
Love lifted me
Love lifted me
When nothing else would help
Love lifted me.*

*God is not unjust; he will not forget your work and the love you have shown him
as you have helped his people and continue to help them.* (14)

And God's Love will lift us every time,
Lift us up to pray.

PRAYER FLOW

Oh LOVE that will not let go of me, I bow before YOU
I bow in weakness;
I bow in submission.
I bow in love.
I want to be a servant known by YOUR LOVE.
Establish my soul to look for YOU.

I will fail.
YOU do not.
Together this love will rise in intercession for others.
I will Love YOU more and then love others through a praying life.
In the Name of Love, Jesus, I submit.

SURGING THOUGHTS

How much do you love God?

Do you understand that prayer is a demonstration of your Love?

What has He done to reveal His Love for you?

Father,
I am seeking
I am hesitant and uncertain,
But will you, O God
Watch over every step of mine
And guide me?

Saint Augustine

A SWEET DISCIPLINE

Such ever was Love's way –
To rise, it stoops

Robert Browning

Chapter Five

LEARNING TO FLOW

Prayer is deliberate.

Deep-to-Deep calls us.
Rivers move with direction and currents carry them.
Elements of weather affect the rushing waters,
But the flow of the river is deliberate.
Oceans create a symphonic sound as crashing waves like cymbals punctuate a dark night or encircle the day with a rolling fluidity spellbinding one's senses as waves heave themselves against the sides of great ships cushioning and yet propelling them forward toward their destination.
Being at sea today I am experiencing this incredible anomaly.
It is an awakening awe.
So constant,
So satisfying,
So predictable.
It is the sensation of being cradled, held by a power of immensity like the grasp of an Eternal Hand.
I am thinking about my husband 's life lived in part at sea on aircraft carriers for thirty years.
What did he hear every day?
Was it a familiar tumultuous roar accompanied by rev'ed up airplane engines working in concert with the ever-moving vessel, which was in perpetual motion most of the time?
Was it a commotion he loved, mixed with the smell of saltwater spray and jet fuel?
Did he relish moments of gazing out upon this massive sphere of water, knowing that the energy it gave off was also a comforting rhythm, a flow of responsible assurance?
A river pulses.
An ocean surges.
Always in motion, a carrier is working with the ocean's movement in a

kind of harmony making a way for the ship to deliver its mission.
They move in relationship, the ship, the man and the ocean.
They move as one.
In the midst of this dynamic flow, there is a deliberate halt when the anchor is dropped.
As it makes its way grudgingly down the side of the ship, the vessel becomes stationary and is grounded, while water continues to circumvent, to flow.
Waters must adjust to position and circumstance.
And so must we.

We have this hope as anchor for the soul, firm and steadfast. (1)

Our position in Christ is an anchor, steadying our lives, bringing to each of us a flow, a deliberate direction.
God's Word is ever challenging our minds, cleansing our hearts, making us *fit* to pray for others, to flow in prayer.
Fit to flow.

Do not be anxious about anything but in everything by prayer and petition with thanksgiving present your requests known unto God.... (2)

There was such a man whose very life flowed in prayer like rivers of many waters.
It also surged like the ocean.
His name was Andrew Murray.
Born in 1828 into a pastor's family in Graaff Reinet, South Africa, Andrew Murray lived in a home filled with prayer, worship and all kinds of interesting people. David Livingston and Robert Moffat, great men of influence and faith would pass through South Africa and stop at the Murray house on their way to somewhere.
Andrew Murray no doubt absorbed life experience through these men, gleaning much from their faith encounters lived out in passion on mission.
We do learn from one another.
A life that flows in prayer is a life in pursuit of God and it is conspicuous.
Someone has to become an example before others.
A praying life has come to believe that prayer changes the world.
Early Christians *met together continually for prayer....* (3)
The Murray household was always occupied with praying people who called down God's Will for others.
Here are Andrew Murray's own words.

"What a mystery and glory there is in prayer? On the one hand we see God in His holiness, love, power, waiting, longing to bless man. On the other hand is…man, a worm of dust bringing down from God by prayer the very life and love of heaven to dwell in his heart. When a man is bold and asks from God what He desires for others…this is the very holiest exercise." (4)

Murray left home at age ten with his brother to study in Scotland, living with his pastor uncle, Reverend John Murray who introduced him to the deep spiritual life and ministry of Robert Burns. This godly man had a great impact and influence upon young Murray. He helped to define Andrew Murray's ministry marking it with" true sincerity, fervent prayer and penetrating preaching… one generation…often waters the seeds of another…." (5)

God positions people before us so we may ascertain truth.

Again Murray's words give us insight.

"Oh, let us begin, as never before to pray for our children, for souls around us, for all the world…because God longs for them and gives us the honor of being the channels through whom His blessing is brought down." (6)

God used his praying life to stir others to pray.

He wrote about prayer, lived prayer, and breathed prayer.

Concerned for women in Holland who were bearing twenty or more children, his first book encouraged them in the rearing of children. This book *Jezus de Kindervriend* appeared in 1858. Murray wrote about the life of Christ written in language adapted to the comprehension of a child.

What a gifted tool this must have been to help guide these large families.

"He possessed the gift of speaking at the right season, the right and just word." (7)

His writing stimulated others to seek a deeper spiritual walk with God and to encompass a praying life. The contribution of his life is still impacting people today for we are reading what he wrote and being aroused and confronted by God's life demonstrated in his.

God delights in raising up standard bearers.

He gives us a riveting account in His Word of another whose life flowed in prayer.

His name was Daniel.

In King Darius's court, the chief of the court officials was a man named Ashpenaz. The king has charged him with the task of bringing some of the Israelites from the royal family into the palace.

Specific criteria were given.

These were to be *young men without any physical defect, handsome, showing aptitude for every kind of learning, well informed, quick to understand and qualified to serve in the king's palace.* (8)

Talk about choosing the *crème de la crème.*

They were selected to learn the language and literature of the Babylonians.

An exceptionally hand picked "focus" group.

Some guidelines were handed out to them.

A certain portion of the king's food and wine were assigned.

They were to be privileged to eat and drink from the king's pantry,

Gourmet not peasant food.

The period of training established for entrance into the king's service was three years.

Daniel had received the mandate but Daniel *knew* he was not to indulge in eating this rich fare.

Because he had great favor with the official, he requested that he and his friends be allowed to eat a simple diet of vegetables and water.

Fearing that Daniel and his friends would become pale and weak the official expressed grave concerns about their appearance and the ramifications that would follow for he was concerned for himself.

Daniel, a young man of discipline, was readied for the ultimatum.

An agreement was struck to allow this diet for ten days.

At the end of the period, the guard would return to see how they looked.

It worked.

They *looked healthier and better nourished than any of the young men who ate the royal food…To these four young men God gave knowledge and understanding of all kinds of literature and learning. And Daniel could understand visions and dreams of all kinds.* (9)

Denial of self had brought great benefit.

It always does.

God was preparing Daniel to flow in prayer.

As Daniel continued to follow a deliberate life of discipline and pursuit of God, trouble began to brew,

A trouble that would attempt to block the vitality of this flow.

He was smart, wise, attractive, responsible, almost perfect, which could have set him up for his own kingdom, not God's.

Chosen to be a satrap, an overseer administrator, he was placed in leadership over his peers.

And a trap was set for him.

His disgruntled competitors fabricated charges against him.

But they were unable to do so…he was trustworthy and neither corrupt or negligent. (10)

Observing his habits of prayer, a plot was hatched.

The plan was to flatter the king into issuing an edict that *any one who prays to any god or man during the next thirty days...shall be thrown into the lion's den.* (11)

Unfortunately the king was skillfully coerced to put it into writing, not knowing Daniel would be the object of its wrath.

When Daniel heard the decree he went into his home where the windows were opened toward Jerusalem.

They were already opened.

And he did what was his custom.

He prayed.

*...Three times a day he got down on his knees and prayed, giving thanks to his God **as he had done before**.* (12)

This was not panic praying.

This was a praying life.

His accusers went back to the king and told of his habit of praying three times a day to his God in spite of the known command signed by the king.

King Darius became distressed and purposed to work feverishly to rescue Daniel in every way he could before sundown.

At last there was no other recourse but to throw him into the lion's den.

The king's words echoed a clarion call for Daniel's God to respond.

May your God whom you serve continually rescue you. (13)

So Daniel entered into his trial

A stone bearing the imprint of the king's ring sealed the opening to the lion's den, documented proof that this act was done with authority.

Now the wait until dawn.

The king spent a miserable night, a night in which he could not eat or sleep, and a night in which he took no amusement for he was greatly troubled.

At the first light of day, he called out to Daniel in an anguished voice, *Daniel, servant of the living God, has your God whom you continually serve, been able to rescue you from the lion's den? Daniel answered, O king, live forever! My God sent his angel, and he shut the mouths of the lions. They have not hurt me, because I was found innocent in his sight...Nor have I ever done any wrong before you.* (14)

Daniel had been delivered.

Envy had been crushed, for his perpetrators instead were destroyed in the lion's den.

Daniel was unharmed for ...no wound was found because he trusted in his God. (15)

King Darius pronounced with great joy these words, which rang throughout the land.

I issue a decree that in every part of my kingdom people must fear and reverence the God of Daniel.

For he is the living God and he endures forever,

His kingdom will not be destroyed,

His dominion will never end.

He rescues and he saves.

He performs signs and wonders in the heavens and on the earth.

He has rescued Daniel... (16)

A life that flows in prayer is a life of risk and rescue.

It was a pleasant February day with a tinge of cold but held by the engaging sunlight streaking through the clouds intermittently, a crisp winter's promise.

I had been packing for a trip with my husband, a personal get away from schedules, daily responsibilities, a time for rest and renewal just for us.

We were so looking forward to this much needed reprieve.

My morning began in prayer.

I felt at peace and was stirred with expectation.

Getting into my car, I began to drive toward the beauty shop, a familiar place.

I planned to park my automobile in a familiar corner spot situated on a grassy knoll.

What occurred next was not at all familiar.

As I approached the parking place, my foot on the brake, a sudden roar surged from the engine and my vehicle lurched out of control, heading over the embankment.

It was a surreal moment.

As the car plummeted into the air, I cried out, "Father, stop the car."

He did.

My foot was still on the brake, holding on when it crashed.

A concrete wall surrounding a garbage dumpster stopped the car.

The sound must have been horrendous, for people came running from everywhere to me.

The automobile was thrust into the air with the front end crumpled like an accordion against the concrete wall.

The rear end was jammed into the small earthy hill.

In effect, the automobile was wedged between the wall and the terraced ground, suspended.

I was stunned, in disbelief but strapped in safely.

Two men rushed to help me climb out.

They had seen the whole ordeal.

After getting me out of the car, we walked over to observe the three feet of tracks burned into the pavement by my tires as I struggled to brake the vehicle.

Shaken but finally succumbing to the realization of what had happened to me, I asked the men to pray with me.

I needed to thank my Father for saving me, for answering my prayer.

We bowed our heads and these were the words that came forth.

"Father I don't understand why, but I know YOU are here. Thank YOU. Prepare Roy for my call to him."

He did.

Roy came and took charge of everything, police, insurance, wrecker and my fragile heart.

A big hug and thoughts of what could have happened was an opportunity for praise to our God.

I could have parked in front of the business and gone through plate glass windows perhaps taking the life of someone else.

But my Father stopped the car.

We did go on our trip in a rental automobile two days later.

God provided all we needed to leave the calamity behind and to trust Him for His provision

I needed stillness, a time for reflection, a processing of what had happened to me.

This scene played in my head for weeks.

For two months there was no automobile to drive.

For two months, I pondered the "how."

For two months, I tried to sort out the "why."

There were no answers except this one.

God allowed it.

He took me through.

He was there.

He is enough.

The unexplained happens,
An ambush,

A diversion,
Some trial.

"These have come so that your faith – of greater worth than gold…may be proved genuine and may result in praise, glory and honor when Jesus Christ is revealed." (17)
A praying life in crisis reveals God because the heart believes He is in it. Amy Carmichael suggests, "Every *trial* is a trust." She quotes The Oxford Dictionary in a new use of the word in 1608 as, "something that serves as an example or proof of a manufacture or material, the skill of an operator…as in a piece of clay by which the progress of the firing (the test) …may be judged as a *trial*-piece." (18)

A trial exposes trust.

I am weak but thou are strong
Jesus keep me from all wrong,
I'll be satisfied as long as I walk,
Let me walk close to Thee.
Just a closer walk with Thee
Grant it Jesus is my plea.
Daily walking close to Thee,
Let it be, dear Lord, let it be.

He will.
When we are deliberate in our choice to stay close to Him with praying lives, there will always be a flow to us of His help, comfort and refuge in all circumstances.

I like garbage dumps now with walls around them.
I park by them on purpose.
I'm glad they are there.
They represent more than someone's refuse.
They are a reminder of a time that an engine surge birthed a prayer surge and my faith had to surge.
I will choose to remember.
Remembering will keep me praying.

PRAYER FLOW

Master of our soul;

We come recognizing the trial and joy of a praying life.
YOU desire to establish our will to pray.
YOU prove your faithfulness
Calamity strikes.
But YOU are present.
Life does have ebb and flow.
We want to live in the flow of YOUR provision, YOUR Grace, YOUR love.
On our own we are inadequate.
Fear is poised to swallow us up
But YOU come.
May our lives receive whatever YOU allow for YOU mean good for us all the days of our lives.
We praise YOU this day with our will.
It is a choice of significance.
We seek to be YOUR disciple, to follow YOU, to be men and women of prayer.
Flow through us to a world that needs to see YOUR power demonstrated in a praying life
In Jesus' Name, we pray for we know YOU will come.

SURGING THOUGHTS

What keeps me from the habit of prayer?

Do I have a hunger for His Presence?

Can I begin today to live a praying life?

**God always answers us in the deeps,
Never in the shallows of our soul.**

Amy Carmichael

Chapter Six

ALTERING YOUR COURSE

Prayer alters.

Like the current in a river, rushing along in a strength born of its existence,
prayer finds its mark.
Changing the course of a river requires radical measures.
Changing course is something we must be prepared do.

Every day something changes.

Weather alters flight schedules.
Traffic congestion causes detours.
Illness cancels plans.
The inexplicable occurs.
God is present when your course changes.

*And this is my prayer; that your love may abound more and more in knowledge
and depth, so that you may be able to discern what is best and may be pure and
blameless until the day of Christ.* (1)

We are all being disciplined to counter when our course takes
an unexpected turn.
Our love for God must be manifested in actions to our fellow man.
We must discern what is best and then act.

BIG TIME

On September 11, 2001 America's way of life was altered forever as terrorism
found its target with two planes deliberately crashing into the Twin Towers
of the World Trade Center in New York City taking them down,
One slamming into the Pentagon in Washington, DC, and one crashing
into a field in Pennsylvania,

On purpose.

Lives were snuffed out.

Great affliction fell upon our land.

Fear stalked.

Shock claimed us.

Sorrow came.

But prayer began to rise.

On September 10th, pastor Jim Cymbala had spent a restless night. He and his wife had experienced an unusually busy Sunday at their church in New York City.

They were tired and needed rest.

However, unable to sleep that evening, he got up to pray and read God's Word.

He was troubled.

Hours began to tick away.

Still disturbed, with no answer, he finally went back to bed.

No sleep would come.

By 5:00 am, he arose again to pray and began to wonder if God was trying to prepare him for something that was coming.

A verse of scripture kept burning inside his heart but it seemed such an odd message.

He who gathers crops in the summer is a wise son, but he who sleeps during harvest is a disgrace. (2)

It seemed to be a verse about harvest, about being ready.

He began soul-searching his heart.

Meditating on this verse, questions came to mind.

"Are we sleeping like that disgraceful son? Am I wasting God's window of opportunity...?" (3)

Seeking God in prayer once more for any lack, asking for forgiveness and insight, he glanced at the clock at 6:20 am and finally fell asleep.

When he awoke, stark chaos had struck his city and altered the course of our nation.

His church opened its arms to 600 new believers the following Sunday.

They were ready.

"The harvest field was ripe with people who suddenly knew at a deep level that they needed God in their lives." (4)

There will always be this need.

There will be defining moments when we know its truth.

I was drawn during the weeks that followed to the despairing faces of men and women displayed on television screens whose families were searching for them.

My heart was burdened for those under the rubble who were crying out for help maybe for the last time.

I carried an ever-present awareness to pray for somebody to come to them, for some word, some piece of music, some angel to reach down to these and give them dying grace.

I could not escape this haunting urgent call.

I prayed for rescue.

I prayed for courage for the families.

I cried out for God's Presence.

It was a consuming vigil for days upon days as our land began to digest the consequence of this horror.

One story that gripped my soul with waves of grief and joy at the same time was the story of Giann Gamboa.

Manager of the Top of The World Cafe located at the top of one of the Towers, he was also a vital part of his church family in Corona, Queens where he lived.

Frequently Giann would begin his day attending the 6:00 am prayer service held at his church. He was known as a man of vibrant faith often taking time to pray with a worried colleague.

"Mr. Gamboa, 26, arranged for 70 children from the church to visit and pray atop the World Trade Center a few months ago...a man who loved being a Christian and sharing his faith with people. The last time any one saw Mr. Gamboa, he was on the 78th floor about to squeeze into a crowded elevator as the building was being evacuated. But he offered his spot instead to a young woman on his staff ...crying and anxious to flee. 'I'll just take the next one,' he told a friend, as the elevator doors shut." (5)

He was a believer in Christ Jesus who responded to need, living out his faith daily before others.

He was positioned to carry the burdens of others even to the surrender of his place to another on the elevator.

He was a mentor, a man who brought children to his business to pray.

As they looked out upon this teeming metropolis, this melting pot of nations, this art, music, theatrical and business center of the world, they prayed for the people.

Prayer matters.

What a view this must have been for them to be perched like an eagle surveying the city, the skyline, and the life they knew.

What an incredible experience to believe that the prayers of children matter and to model prayer before them.

What did the prayers of 70 children do to prepare this city for the oncoming disaster?

Did they alter its course?

Did they have any effect upon the people?

They did.

Remember how the people of New York came together to help, to pray, to give, to operate in solidarity as *one body*?

God was present.

He is always in the midst of suffering.

Two steel beams came crashing down out of the rubble a few days later.

When they fell, crossing one another they landed as if fused together into the shape of a mammoth Cross.

The picture of this phenomenon found its way into newspapers across our land including my own.

Did it just happen?

People were drawn to it daily at Ground Zero as they prepared for the staggering work ahead of recovery.

They went to pray.

It was as if a jagged makeshift altar had been dropped down out of the wreckage into the midst of altered shattered lives,

A presence.

God is present in crisis.

Prayer is a work of God.

And it flowed.

The children had prepared the way.

Carry each others burdens, and in this way you will fulfill the law of Christ. (6)

We are to enter into the life of prayer wherever and whenever God directs us.

Thomas Merton said, "God came to us because God wanted to join us on the road, to listen to our story, and to help us realize that we are not walking in circles but moving toward the house of peace and joy."

We join people on the road through prayer.

Prayer encompasses the stories of others.

Prayer gripped this nation.

God summoned his people to pray.

Too soon we tend to forget and must relearn what we thought we knew

how to do.
One never graduates from the school of prayer.
Our course will constantly be altered.

On December 26, 2004, an unearthly sound was heard as our world awakened to the most potent earthquake in forty years. It struck under the Indian Ocean in Indonesia about 100 miles off the coast of Sumatra, triggering massive tsunami waves that obliterated villages and cities, seaside resorts, leaving in its wake, tens of thousands of people who lost their lives. It swept across the Indian Ocean with a fury from Thailand to Somalia. These giant waves are the results of volcanic eruptions or earthquakes. Energy creates an initial wave that splits into two, one moves out into the ocean while the other heads for shore. There can be speeds of up to 500 mph. When it reaches the shoreline, it forms walls of water called bores. (7)
Every scene depicted in our media was filled with people running for their lives, people drowning, and people being washed out to sea.
Homes and hotels were slammed and lifted away by these killer waves.
What a cry went out to God all over the world as we began to seek Him.
Water, food, shelter were desperate needs.
Prayer and action found a way to reach out.
My pastor felt compelled to respond, to do something to aid the victims.
Quickly a team from our church assembled and on January 6th they flew to the island of Sumatra carrying their own supplies of food, water and tents.
He was asked the question, "Why have you come?"
"Because I am a follower of Jesus, He loves them."
A verse of scripture, birthed in prayer was given to them for this mission and its message burned in their hearts as they traveled to this place of anguish.
Who will not fear you, O Lord and bring glory to our name?
For you alone are holy.
All nations will come and worship before you.... (8)
Love is a rallying call.
People must *see* love in action.
This team of people heard a call to go and altered their plans.
Bodies needed burying, a water treatment plant was priority, a helping hand.
Other groups went for weeks afterwards.
People were signing up to go.
Why?

God changed our course.

Graphic reports obtained by journalists who interviewed people from the demolished regions were heart wrenching.

"…You keep running…until the water lifts you off your feet and sweeps you onward. It makes no difference whether you can swim or not. The force carries you forward, and you become a living, breathing projectile." (9)

People grabbed posts, trees, anything and hung on for life.

The moving walls of water carried people from area to area, emptying out hotel pools, catapulting automobiles through the air, and destroying all.

The magnitude of this tsunami force staggered comprehension.

But prayer began to surge across this world with tidal waves of faith enveloping the tormented lives with love.

One inspiring account documented by the charitable organization called The Barnabus Fund is as follows:

"On December 26, Reverend Dayalan Sanders, founder of a Christian orphanage in Sri Lanka, heard a terrible roar from the sea and saw the first of the waves approaching. He only had time to scream out in Tamil the word, *evacuate*. There was nowhere to go but seaward. Thirty-five small children plus Sanders piled into a boat meant for six. Amidst the cries of the children, Sanders called out in the name of the Lord for safety. He remembered words from Isaiah; 'I will deliver you from the elements because my standard is over you.' Yes, they were saved. Onlookers from the shore were in amazement. It was a miracle."

Indeed we are called to pray.

Praying the Word of God in catastrophe necessitates knowing it.

This pastor had made part of the fabric of his life.

The habit of prayer in a life rises up and takes us where God leads.

"Have courage for the great sorrows of life and patience for the small ones; and when you have laboriously accomplished your daily tasks, go to sleep in peace. God is awake."
Henri Nowen

God does not sleep.

Let Him have all your worries and cares, for He is always thinking about you and watching everything that concerns you. (10)

When peace like a river attendeth my way,

When sorrow like sea billows roll,
Whatever my lot.
Thou has taught us to say
It is well,
It is well with my soul.

The writers of our hymns knew we would need solace in the midst of the storm.
They knew that it was found in Christ alone.
Circumstances will change.
Our God remains.

Prayer matters to God.
It is the surge in faith.

PRAYER FLOW

Giver of Life;
Who birthed creation in all its intrinsic beauty and potential.
We are in awe of YOUR magnitude
YOU, Oh Lord know what is coming into our lives.
YOU turn tragic consequences into opportunities for good will.
Danger will come but we will experience YOU in the midst of it.
We must carry hope to the hopeless.
YOUR PRESENCE will guide us through.
Give us a mind and heart of readiness.
Inspire us to give ourselves in prayer for others.
Prevailing prayer is a mighty fortress, a wall of refuge against which waves of destruction and hardship flail fruitlessly.
It will rise up to aid the weak and broken.
Help us to be that wall for someone today.
We will depend upon YOU,
Author and Finisher of our faith
All Sufficient Jesus
In YOUR NAME ALONE, I pray.

SURGING THOUGHTS

How does God use prayer when disaster strikes?

Does my prayer make a difference?

Is the habit of prayer a first response or a last resort when need arises?

> To clasp the hands in prayer is the beginning
> Of an uprising against the disorder of the world.
>
> Karl Barth

A DELIBERATE DIRECTION

Lord take my heart,
For I cannot give it to you.
And when you have it,
Keep it.
For I would not take it from you.

Francois Fenelon

Chapter Seven

PRAYER TO SAVE

Surging prayer lifts.

There is ebb and flow to a praying life, a surge.
Webster's dictionary gives us dimensions to the word "surge."
It defines "surge" as a heavy billowing motion like that of great waves or a sudden onrush, a ground swell, a tumultuous rising and falling." Coming from the Latin word *surgere*, it means to "lead straight up, to rise up from below, to lead, rule."
As we visualize the image of an ocean surging, we explore the words "ebb and flow."
The ebb is the "period between high water and low water," a decrease.
The flow is the "rising of the tide," an increase.
In the ebb and flow of a praying life, the call for *saving* prayer comes.
The people of God respond to the call.
Why?
It is urgent.
They are seasoned in responding.
They know it is imperative.
They are accountable.
This is the work left for us to do.

A prayer surge:

Saves
Undergirds
Releases
Galvanizes
Encounters

God's Word counsels us.

Build, build up! Make a road!
Clear the way; remove the rocks from the road my people will travel.
A Message from the high and towering God,
who lives in eternity
whose name is Holy:
'I live in the high and holy places,
But also with the low spirited, the spirit-crushed,
And what I do is put new spirit in them, get them up and on their feet again.' (1)

Prayer clears the road of obstacles, makes a way for the broken and crushed
to be lifted up again.
How important is lifting the spirit of another?
Very.
"You know some things don't matter that much…like the color of a house,
But lifting a person's heart, now that matters…The hardest thing on earth
is choosing what matters." (2)
Prayer matters.
Surging prayer exhibits confidence in God.

There are moments of extremity in which we must cry out.

In 1968, in Vietnam, while serving with the US Navy, my fighter pilot
husband was shot down in his F4 Phantom jet and had to eject over rough
seas.
He cried out.
God heard his prayer and saved him
A *saving* prayer.
A helicopter was scrambled from the carrier to reach him.
Roy was wrapped up in parachute lines, struggling to survive.
His back seat radar intercept officer ejected and popped up in an upright
position.
The rescue pilot did not know that one was in danger and one was not.
He *just happened* to choose Roy first.
He needed *saving* literally.
My husband is alive today because of that prayer.
As a young teenaged boy of sixteen he and his father wrote a country song
about prayer.
Here is the first verse.

I Call Him
Well the blue's still in the water and the blue's still in the sky
And way beyond the blue there's someone watchin' from on high
Well, my clothes may be ragged and my shoes may be worn
But I've been a wealthy boy since I've been born
Cause I call Him when I'm troubled and I call Him when I'm weak
And he always pulls me through my troubles some way and I believe
He'll be there (he'll be there) he'll be there (he'll be there)
Like He always is to answer
When I call Him.

And He was.
God was preparing Roy for a praying life even then.

We are building up the road for others when we pray.
Obstacles block vision.
They obscure God.
We are conduits of His Love.

But you dear friends build yourselves up in your most holy faith. Pray in the Holy Spirit. Keep yourselves in God's love. (3)

The Spirit of God becomes our guide to living. He is operating in our lives because we belong to Jesus.
The Spirit directs because we call for help.
God's Spirit beckons. There are things to do.... (4)
Prayer is one of them.

If we don't know how or what to pray, it doesn't matter, He does our prayer in and for us making prayer out of wordless sighs and groans. (5)

So prayer comes forth by God's Spirit.
Theologically He has given us the way to pray.
The Spirit of God urges us on.
How does keeping us connected to God's Love build up faith and therefore the journey for someone else?
Living for Him compels us to seek what He loves.
Since God cares about people, praying for them pleases Him and reinforces their faith.
Prayer removes the boulder in the road.
When we are urged by His Spirit to pray for another, our cry becomes a saving prayer.

In effect, we will *snatch others...and save them.* (6)

Saving prayer must be prayed in the Name of Jesus.

And I will do whatever you ask in my name.... (7)

It is in His Name alone, prayer is validated.

There are times we are prompted to unite in prayer, to cry out for others as one voice.

One March evening a special night of prayer was diligently planned as women came together in a rural community in South Carolina to receive encouragement from God's Word and to be inspired to pray it.
I was privileged to be the leader.
There were many church affiliations represented but One God present in our midst loving us. How His Spirit flowed, moving heart to heart drawing women to Himself.
Springtime in Summerton, South Carolina was showing up everywhere in containers of perky bright daffodils and baskets of rich scarlet geraniums.
Nature was taking hold and announcing the beauty of God's handiwork.
It was evidenced on this night as we gathered to partake of a scrumptious southern meal prepared by women who wanted to give their best and did so.
We feasted on home cooked fresh vegetables of every kind, Kentucky Wonders, pole beans, succulent squash casserole, copper penny carrots and sumptuously sampled southern desserts of praline cake, richly decadent pecan pie and home made custard banana pudding.
We tasted of the goodness of God but there was more to taste.
Never have I experienced such a movement of affirmation from an audience.
Waves of God's Love punctuated sentences with sigh, smiles and nodding heads in agreement. Indeed He was removing roadblocks found in the hearts of the women.
We needed to be of one mind and heart to surge in prayer together.
We had been called to pray for several hundred men who were assembling for a sporting event held in a barn not far away.
A speaker would be challenging them to live a life of faith.
A pastor had asked us to pray for this meeting
After coming into worship through music, I began to share the impact of prayer in my life.

We then opened our Bibles to Psalm 112.
We were going to pray the Word of God as our prayer, our saving prayer for these men.

Blessed is the man who fears the Lord, who finds great delight in his commands....
(8)

We began to read out loud and pray this psalm making it our prayer of consensus.
Some of these men had never considered God's place in their lives.
Surely a man is blessed who comes to God and becomes His child.
A man's legacy is vital.
We then prayed that, *his children will be mighty in the land, the generation of the upright will be blessed.* (9)
A blessed man with blessed children.
We asked God to prosper him.
The Word of God says that such a man has *wealth...in his house and righteousness forever.* (10)
For the acquiring pursuit of riches becomes more than just an obstacle on the road.
It becomes a god.

> If a man does not serve God
> He will make a god to serve.
> C S Lewis

Wealth is an effective servant, a poor god.
Deep in the heart, men know if this goal has edged out God Almighty.
They understand.
Saving prayer clears the road, paving the way for liberty and insight.
Mark Twain profoundly said, "It's not the things I do not understand that bother me. It's the things I do understand."
Saving prayer breaks down the walls of the heart so one can hear from God.
This sanctuary of women was a sensitive voice crying out to God for their men.
We continued to pray the scripture, *even in darkness, light dawns (for this man) For the upright, for the compassionate, righteous man.* (11)
Women want their husbands to be gracious, compassionate, righteous, and able to discern the right thing to do even in darkness.
This was farming country.

Cotton and corn had been planted recently and there had been a few days of very chilly temperatures dipping below the norm. Farmers were anxious at the possible effect of change in weather upon their crops.
We prayed for the harvest, for God's Hand upon them, for abundance.
We asked that ...*good would come to him who is generous and lends freely.*(12)
We finished the entire psalm...that he would *conduct his affairs with justice,* that ...*he would never be shaken... be remembered forever.* That he would have *no fear of bad news....* That his heart would be *secure...looking in triumph on his foes* and because *he has scattered his gifts (good will) to the poor, his righteousness endures forever; his horn will be lifted high in honor.* (13)

These verses image a man much beloved, admired, sought after, a just man who raises the standard, a stable man who is generous, productive, a leader remembered, one who is not afraid of bad news, a man of integrity who is vindicated before his accusers, a man of God.
Do you think this is an effective prayer for a man?
It was the Word of God, prayed at twilight by believing women with burning hearts, earnest for God's intervention.
And He did.
Men were snatched from themselves by a loving God coming to meet them on the road of disillusionment and discouragement.
They were restored unto their Maker and then to their families.
We had surged in prayer as one voice, one faith, and one heart unto God.
And so indeed we are called to build up the road of faith through prayer, clearing it of barriers, rocks, and hindrances so that the Holy God who loves each one can reach down and lift the heart of the pilgrim in need.
Surging prayer saves.
It is prayer that does "lead straight up" rising to lift up someone before the throne of a
Loving God who is waiting to answer.

Oh, souls are you weary and troubled?
No light in the darkness you see.
There's light for a look at the Savior
And life more abundant and free
Turn your eyes upon Jesus,
Look full in His wonderful face
And the things of earth will grow strangely dim
In the light of His Glory and Grace.

The Lord is gracious and righteous;
Our God is full of compassion.

The Lord protects the simplehearted;
When I was in great need, he saved me. (14)

In *saving* prayer we cry out in Jesus' Name, empowered by the Holy Spirit. And He comes.

PRAYER FLOW

Overcoming Father;
YOU are present when we come as many and pray as one voice.
YOU long for us to bond in unity, to believe YOU will hear.
Thank YOU for allowing us to experience this kind of praying.
We want to please YOU.
Cleanse our hearts from any boulders of our own.
Fill us afresh and anew with YOUR Spirit.
Strengthen our resolve to keep clearing the road of faith for the people of God.
Awaken us; bring a detour, a call, and an urgency by YOUR Spirit.
Lives need saving every day.
Something eternally wonderful happens as a group assembles before YOU.
Remind us to be faithful, to be in YOUR Word, to realize we can pray it as our prayer. Give us *saving* words to cry out to YOU for others.
YOU alone save,
In Jesus' Name, I pray

SURGING THOUGHTS

When was the last time you were drawn with others to pray together for a specific focus?

Is scripture an effective prayer?

Will you purpose to be present to God when a call for saving prayer comes?

Lord, Come to me, my door is open
Michel Quoist

Chapter Eight

PRAYER TO UNDERGIRD

Surging prayer strengthens.

For the eyes of the Lord range throughout the earth to strengthen those whose hearts are fully committed to Him. (1)

To undergird is to "strengthen from beneath."
Our God knows when we need to be strengthened.
He calls people to pray just for this reason.

It was a crisp January evening that felt like an "after Christmas slump."
The blahs had begun to settle in and find a home.
I awakened with a deep sinus congestion, which clung to me for days.
Finally the blahs succumbed to a beleaguering virus.
Misery had entered.
For two weeks, my days and nights ran together.
Fever seemed to dissipate in the mornings and rose with the midnight watch.
At night I could not breathe.
Sleep eluded.
Exhaustion was making her bed.
In the daytime I was weakened from the evening battle to inhale through the blocked nasal passages.
The third week in January, I was scheduled to speak to a group in a church in Jackson, Tennessee known as the "YaDa Sisterhood."
About ten days before I was to come, I called Lisa their leader and explained how ill I was.
I asked for prayer, knowing that God uses prayer to make a way for us.
Lisa and I had connected on several occasions about this event.
Prayer was at the heart of the YaDa group.
Prayer strengthens.
It undergirds.
Immediately I was placed before the prayer team for the next ten days.

I wanted God's Will
Sometimes the plan is changed.

I desire to do your will, O my God. (2)

Lisa felt God's Hand leading her during the fall of 2004 to pull together an organization for women that would meet monthly to foster fun and fellowship but also feed their faith. The name "YaDa" was chosen, for in Hebrew it means, *"to know"* God.
This is the explanation printed on the front of the YaDa Tee shirts:
"Yada" verb (Strong's 3045), *"to know"*
To know God is to have intimate experiential knowledge of Him…to serve Him…to trust Him…." (3)
Knowing Christ circumscribes all of life, the good and the bad days.
He knew we would need supernatural strength to go through, His strength.

Yet it was the Lord's will to crush him and cause him to suffer. (4)

The mighty access of strength was provided through the life of Jesus.
He was crushed.
And life crushes us.
Our alignment with Him through relationship is the source of strength we need.
Prayer aligns.
Women had come alongside Lisa, catching the vision of intercepting women in the crossroads of daily living and strengthening them.
I knew if I did not have a healing effort in prayer, I would not be present at this occasion.
Within the next three to four days, my doctor ordered a sinus shot to shrink swollen membranes and I was counseled to be on vocal rest for 24 hours.
That part was easy.
Yes, I was in prayer from the first day of this illness.
I wanted to be where God wanted me to be.
One thing I learned long ago from scripture is this: when we pray we are to thank God for whatever the situation is, in distress, in discomfort, even in illness.
This is an act of the will, a choice.
Why?

Because God tells us to do so.

Pray continually; give thanks in all circumstances, for this is God's Will for you in Christ Jesus. (5)

Answers began to evolve.
My husband Roy decided to take off from work and drive me to Jackson, another answer to prayer, as it is an hour's trip both ways.
I knew I was unable to have mental or physical stamina for driving.
I had prayed for God to reveal His Way.
It now seemed apparent.
I was to go.
I knew I would not have the strength I needed to communicate the message I had prepared until it was time to give it.
When I arrived at the church, to my surprise there was an incredible energy and anticipation in the flow of the evening as expectant women were bustling everywhere handling details.
I breathed in possibility out of impossibility.
The committee of YaDas serve in a variety of ways, some secure door prizes donated from businesses which are given away, some cook dishes for the delicious pot luck dinner, all give. Guests are greeted by lively music playing *We Are Family* and hostesses dressed in YaDa Tee shirts paired with casual attire.
It was obvious to me that I had been undergirded in prayer, carried and brought to this place.
After the meal, I excused myself and went to the ladies room to be alone to pray.
I overheard two women who were newcomers saying, "Well there is no good place to dance in Jackson so we decided to come here tonight."
I smiled inside.
A Creative God had orchestrated their coming.
I was dancing already.
I knew why I had been raised up to come.
A mature lady stood and prayed for me before I spoke.
God's Presence came.
Strength surged through me bringing a holy pardon to an aching body.
Surging prayer had strengthened me.
It was as though momentarily I stepped outside of myself.
The topic was "Peace in the Storm" and rolling waves of peace washed over me as I spoke and a greater liberty engulfed me.

It was God's Will to prepare me to speak through illness,
In weakness.
Riplets of faith surged like the rush of a river through hearts as fresh faith
poured out upon these women, strengthening them to continue, to believe
God, to belong, to do His Will, to be thankful in all circumstances.
Tears flowed.
Joy was restored.
The road was cleared for me.
Prayer makes a way.

For it is God who works in you to will and to act according to His good purpose.
(6)

We are to pray continually, thanking Him, asking for His Will.
Then we are to do His Will.
Sometimes it will be costly.
"It is true, his sheep do know his voice. We can safely trust him to lead us
and not let us make a mistake if we really want to do his will." (7)

> Worry does not empty tomorrow of sorrow
> It empties today of its strength.
> Corrie Ten Boom

Pass me not, O gentle Savior,
Hear my humble cry;
While on others Thou art calling,
Do not pass me by.
Savior, Savior, hear my humble cry,
While on others Thou are calling,
Do not pass me by.

Weakness was good for me.
It will be good for you as well.
Weakness will come.
But our God looks far and wide to find a heart seeking after Him.
He will find us.
Dependent,
Undergirded,
Surging in prayer, we strengthen another because He is our strength.

PRAYER FLOW

Loving Father;
We need the arms of faith to enfold us, to strengthen us for the tasks
ahead.
We long to bring an offering of love to YOU.
We would not knowingly choose weakness.
Illness diminishes resolve.
YOU always know the whole picture.
Setbacks set us back
Sometimes we want to give up, quit.
YOU want us to ask for YOUR Will in the matter, to attempt more than
we are able.
We call for help.
Praying hearts carry us through.
YOU want to demonstrate YOUR Love.
Every time we choose to stay the course, we surge in belief and our faith is
enlarged, strengthened.
Somebody receives because somebody prayed.
I will choose to believe,
Because of Jesus in whose Name is my strength.

SURGING THOUGHTS

How does the prayers of others strengthen us?

Do you really want the Will of God?

Is there someone right now that needs your prayer?

Behold my needs which I know not myself
Francois Fenelon

Chapter Nine

PRAYER TO RELEASE

Surging Prayer resists.

"Prayer is an inner battlefield on which the issues of character are settled…
when a man… thirsting after righteousness, calls God into alliance, he
does so because he has a fight on his hands" (1)
The heart is where character forms.
Prayer is a decision of the will.
There are days when attempts to pray for another cannot rise because we
are bogged down in our own.
Blocked by obstacles of our own making.
We rationalize and negotiate the *whys*…
Worry has its weights.
Thoughts betray.
Other voices thwart.

No one cares.
Unkind words.
Wounded.
Angry.
Let down.
No one understands.
Dissipated dreams.
Alone.
Unfit,
Ugly,
No one listens.
A dreaded darkness descends, drawing us down, closing in.
Distractions,
Diversions,
Defeating prayer.

Losing touch with God is a downward spiral.
We begin to slip away from prayer.
It will cost us too much.
To pray one must face his own heart and ask God to reveal what is there,
to intervene.
If we ask Him to come, He will.
He reminds us of His availability.

Do not fear...I am with you...I will help you. (2)

Our walled compromises can erect a barricade.
Deciding to focus on feelings causes us to step back from God.
Faith is factual.
Prayer is the channel through which our faith receives oxygen.
It breathes through walls.
When a hardened, desensitized heart ignores God, we discover we are
unable to pray.

Today if you hear his voice, do not harden your hearts. (3)

Hearts rebel.
Life is not about you or me.
It's about God.
Prayer is our divine link to Him.
Asking Him to come to the rescue is to begin to resist.
What?
Building blocks of apathy and selfishness.
Prayerlessness separates us from God.
It is a boulder on the highway of faith.
Prayerlessness is sin.
Confession is not ritual but release.

If we confess our sins, he is faithful and just and will forgive us... (4)

Know your sin, your own boulders.
One by one they must be removed, daily.
Some are easy to declare.
Some challenge.
Some gasp to hang on.
All must go.

Sin separates.
Cleansed once again we are released, we can pray.
A Holy God requires a clean heart.

He looks at the heart (5)
Create in me a pure heart and renew a steadfast spirit within me. (6)

Others have struggled with these dark forces that oppose a deepening relationship to God through prayer not fully comprehending the role of a clean heart.
The Spirit of the Living God urges us to take up, to resist, and return, to know release.
Henri Nowen prayed, "Dear Lord, give me a growing desire to pray. It remains so hard for me to give my time generously to you. I am still greedy for time – time to be useful, effective, successful, time to excel, produce. But you, O Lord, ask nothing but my simple presence, my humble recognition of my nakedness, my **defenseless confession of my sins**, so that you can let the rays of your love enter my heart and give me the deep knowledge that I can love because you have loved me first…. What holds me back? What makes me so hesitant and stingy, so careful and calculating? Do I still doubt that I need nothing beside you? Please, Lord, help me to give up these immature games, and let me love you freely, boldly, courageously and generously." (7)

Released from self-absorption, we can pray,
Released from the me that hides Thee,
Released to love another through prayer.
Neutralizing our faith through prayerlessness shuts down this powerful call.
"No one can unclutter his life without uncluttering his heart." (8)
Clean hearts are an ongoing work of confession.
To pray is to enter the spiritual arena of life fortified.
There is an inner battlefield.
Prayer is a weapon.

The Bible speaks of *the weapons we wield* and they are *not merely human, but divinely potent to demolish strongholds…* (9)

Strongholds are walled entrenchments of resistance to Truth in our lives.
God gives us His Word as a way through these attacks and His Spirit to

bring us resolution.

Elisabeth Elliot was dallying with doubts about the effect of prayer until she read God's Word. She said, "The source of my doubts about its potency was not the Holy Spirit…it was the unholy spirit, the destroyer himself, urging me to quit using the weapon he fears so intensely." (10)

To capture our hearts and keep us from prayer is a strategy of darkness.

Darkness comes to torment the heart of the believer, to destroy prayer, to destroy you.

The Bible tells us there is an adversary to be acknowledged.

He is described as a roaring lion, (11)

He prowls around looking for a victim, a ruler of darkness, (12)

He brings darkness, a tempter, (13)

He lures us away from God.

There are many names for him in God's Word.

To me, he is the enemy of the soul.

He hates a clean heart.

Why?

Because prayer that knows how to resist him defeats him.

So how do we respond when we find ourselves sliding into disbelief, swayed by feelings of helplessness, side tracked from our true heritage?

We resist…and he must flee. (14)

We resist in prayer, empowered by a clean heart.

Stopping the flow and work of prayer is a mission of the enemy of your soul.

Prayer is God's weapon of authority.

It breaks through because it breaks down resistance.

Our God loves a praying heart.

We rise in faith when we pray.

He rises by lifting others
Robert G. Ingersoll

Prayer lifts us so we can lift others to the Savior.

…The prayer of the upright is his delight. (15)

He knew we would be in a battle of good and evil that would vie for our hearts.

Prayer delights Him.

"…The prayers of the upright are an extension and outworking of the heart...the heart of the upright magnifies the power and grace of God. The prayer of the upright is a delight to God because it expresses those affections of the heart which call attention to the all- sufficient God." (16)

Indeed HE is All Sufficient, Loving, Forgiving, and Able.

Prayer is an offering to Him.

And HE is watching.

For the eyes of the Lord are on the righteous and his ears are attentive to their prayers but the face of the Lord is against those who do evil. (17)

Evil does not win;

But it battles to win.

So we must enter with strategy.

How can we be readied?

Through a heart made clean by confession.

Through a heart of praise and thanksgiving,

Praise is an integral part of prayer's arsenal.

Darkened hearts cannot praise because sin blocks it.

Praise parts the darkness.

"I had been beginning my days with petition. I should have been beginning them with praise." (18)

When prayer is shut down we begin to think only about what we do not have.

Praise is worship and it ushers in God's Presence causing promises to flow again.

It is the music of true intimacy.

Worship the Lord with gladness; Come before him with joyful songs. Know that the Lord is good. It is he who made us, and we are his...enter his gates with thanksgiving and his courts with praise; give thanks to him and praise his name. (19)

Clean hearts want to praise their God with thanksgiving.

Clean hearts acknowledge the empowering Word of God.

Clean hearts remember that the Blood of Jesus is the covering of ownership over them.

Clean hearts can stand firm against any foreboding darkness and neutralize its influence through prayer.

Clean hearts have authority over evil.

This is an overcoming life.
Prayer becomes the proving ground for emerging faith.
Prayer battles are real.
Combat comes.

It was turning out to be an exceptionally, warm October in New York City.
My daughter Kellye was there for a photo shoot with a magazine.
I was there to pray for her and absorb the city's heartbeat, to enjoy.
My first stop was Central Park.
Just a sprinkling of golden and crimson tinged leaves had fallen.
Finding my way to a weathered bench, with paper in hand, I drank in the sounds of the city; billboarded taxis honking incessantly, sirens screeching in the distance, a slight breeze rustling through the branches of an oak tree. It was an inviting welcome as a resplendent sun winked intermittently. Small children were giggling as they chased each other while playing a game of tag; young lovers were basking in a familiar embrace, unaware of the world around them. There was a stand-off in progress as a prissy champagne colored poodle adorned with pink bows tried to avoid the sleek black doberman's sharp eye and low ominous growl while the owners of these dogs frantically clung to their leashes. A gentle elderly couple clad in comfortable old clothes walked slowly, arm in arm, while a young man clad in kneepads and a blue helmet, roller bladed by them, oblivious.
Striking vignettes of lives in seasons.
This park obviously was an oasis for the city folks.
Greenery, beauty, roots, space.
Vitality and tranquility in the same place.
I sent up a quiet prayer for the people as they passed by me.
I asked for a God awareness of the Creator to be born in each one as they embraced this autumn day He had created for them.
They were enjoying a lovely escape, a delightful reprieve, and personal refreshment. People do need to stop, look and listen.
I was invigorated when I left.
I thanked God for my time there.
The next leg of my day took me to Macy's department store.
It was a mere dash of twenty-four blocks and I managed to work up a bit of an appetite.
Along the way, people were taking in the day's gift of warm weather as they lunched at outdoor patio cafes, sipping lattes and conversing about life.
As I walked, the smells of ethnic food were tempting.

Variety and diversity was to be had for the asking, a smorgasbord of food.

Vendors displayed their wares on every street corner, colorful souvenir shirts with New York logos, costume jewelry from around the world, local artistic renderings representative of the city's sights and fashionable handbags for the right price.

Policemen were visible everywhere and they were courteous.

All through the day I prayed for Kellye asking God for His blessing upon her.

To my amazement, I only bought one thing at Macy's, a shopping bag, and then visited the *Miracle on Thirty Fourth Street* exhibit complete with photos of little Natalie Wood on display.

I ambled back stopping for coffee, relishing my afternoon.

Upon returning to our hotel, I discovered that we had been moved to the twenty first floor. The air conditioning was not working in our room and the temps were soaring for October. Kellye called me and related her day which was filled with the stresses of twelve hours associated with photography; makeup, hair, clothes, attitudes.

It had not been an easy or pleasant task.

She was spent and disenchanted.

God sometimes allows us to be right in the middle of circumstances that are difficult because He wants someone who loves Him to be there, to be an influence.

The good news is this: He's there too.

The next two days included interesting jaunts to 9/11 Ground Zero, a Broadway musical and a late night rendezvous with some of her friends who work in the city.

We had planned an early breakfast the last day in order to accommodate a lengthy ride across town to the airport.

However, one more adventure awaited us.

Rising early we were packed and ready to go have breakfast by 8 o'clock.

We boarded the elevator on our floor, the twenty first.

Five other people joined us: a flirtatious young couple in their twenties who were affectionate and demonstrative, a tall, muscular African-American man who looked like a pro athlete, a smartly attired bespeckled business woman who had a rolling suitcase in hand and a small woman with a pensive face and disheveled hair carrying a brown jacket.

I don't ordinarily notice people in such a detailed way while in an elevator but the seconds usually experienced as an elevator descends became lengthy minutes.

As it approached the seventeenth floor, there was a jolt followed by a deafening thud.

It seemed to lurch and then stopped abruptly.

We knew immediately, we were not going anywhere for a while.

The lights flickered and then emergency lighting came on.

We were trapped.

I then began to observe everything around me.

Guess what?

The elevator was decorated, yes, decorated in a draped patterned material in shades of chocolate, light and dark.

We were cocooned in designer fabric and it was getting warmer with every passing moment.

The size of the elevator seemed adequate for the number of people in it but one more would have made it unbearably cramped.

Within seconds the people began to react.

The efficient businesswoman picked up the phone on the wall and called the desk to alert them.

Her tone of voice was low key but had a controlled edge as she said, "Are you aware that there is a group of us on the seventeenth floor in an elevator that is stuck?"

The answer came back, "yes, we are aware."

She then said, "Do you have an engineer?"

"Yes, we do."

Her query continued, "Is he in the city or is he in the building?"

"He is in the building."

That was all of the conversation.

Every one now settled into their spot to wait.

There was a restless uncertain silence that followed as we hung somewhere between floors, suspended, wondering how long we would be there.

I was in the back corner of the left side.

Kellye was in the back corner of the right side.

Somehow we had gotten separated when we got into the elevator.

The tall African-American man who was between us seemed quiet, observant as though he was analyzing the situation.

The businesswoman who initiated communication with the hotel was stationed in front, left of the elevator door.

The couple standing to the right of the elevator door in front had now pulled apart from their embrace, disgruntled, sighing, complaining, exasperated at their bad fortune.

The small anxious woman who stood between the businesswoman and me looked as though she might faint for she began to wring her hands together.

I spoke and asked Kellye if she was all right because she had awakened this morning with the beginnings of a migraine.

She said, "I'm ok" and closed her eyes.

I knew she was praying. As the temperature started to rise, we began to peel off any layers of clothing that were feasible.

The stifling air was being used up.

I sensed a repugnant smothering oppression surrounding us. A wall of deep anxiety was building; fear was trying to establish a foothold.

It was the angst of helplessness that the enemy of your soul delivers when misfortune knocks.

I knew what I must do.

I began to pray out loud but softly, calling on Jesus, thanking Him for Who He is, asking for help, for release.

I prayed for trust and calmness for the people in this elevator.

Just praying penetrated the heaviness in the air for it was a resistance to the overwhelming predicament.

We became aware of our breath as if by so doing, we could conserve oxygen.

Beads of perspiration began to form on my brow.

The minutes ticked off laboriously.

No other words were spoken,

Just me praying.

The tentative woman who was wringing her hands relaxed and moved physically next to me as I continued to pray.

It was as if a shelter had been provided for her inner soul.

Prayer is a shelter.

Eleven minutes passed in an unearthly stillness and then without any warning, suddenly the doors spontaneously opened.

Instantly every one spilled out.

No one said goodbye.

No one knew each other's names.

It was a release I shall never forget.

As a joke, Kellye said, "Mom, do you want to wait for another elevator?"

I cracked a smile and said, "No, thanks."

Momentum restored, we bounded hilariously down seventeen floors like we were on the wings of a dove.

It was easy.

An unseen Hand whisked us all the way to the bottom.

Hungry now, once we got to the lobby, we asked for directions to the hotel restaurant.

We entered without speaking, sat down and tried to collect our thoughts.

Corralled on the seventeenth floor in an elevator with five other people.
No one panicked.
Fear came.
Faith overcame.
Delivered.
Released.
Grateful.
Safe.
The waitress came over and asked us how we were.
We said, "Fine, now."
She inquired further.
"We were in the elevator on the seventeenth floor that was stuck."
"Oh, we heard about that, sorry, glad you are out, in fact I think the hotel should buy you breakfast."
We shrugged our shoulders and in a few minutes she had arranged it.
Breakfast was scrumptious.
The ride to the airport was exhilarating.
God was in His Heavens and all seemed right with the world.
But for eleven minutes He was locked up with us in an elevator.
He heard our cry, dispelled the darkness, broke through and released us.
"We must learn to pray far more for spiritual victory…for God's greatest gift – spiritual triumph. This triumph is not deliverance from, but victory in, trial, and that not intermittent but perpetual." (20)
We experience spiritual triumph when we see God in the situation.
There will be days of trouble and turmoil.
There will be delays and disappointments,
The unexpected and the unexplained will come.
And so will He.
We must resist the enemy of our soul by developing bedrock, persevering faith that unashamedly calls out for rescue to a God who answers.
A power surge brought a blackout.
A prayer surge bought His Presence to an elevator of strangers who were locked up together.
Once again the words of an old hymn weave the message of God's provision to us.

I must tell Jesus all of my trials.
I cannot bear these burdens alone,
In my distress He kindly will help me.
He ever loves and cares for His own.

I must tell Jesus....

I did.

Before they call I will answer;
While they are still speaking I will hear. (21)

He heard.
He is the power surge.
Prayer is the weapon of release.

PRAYER FLOW

Holy Deliverer;
YOU are the Hightower I run into when I am afraid.
YOU hear my cry.
I ask for YOUR GRACIOUS HAND of mercy to open the door of my heart this day.
There are boulders on my path that must be removed.
They hide YOU.
Some are of my own making.
Some are from the adversary.
I have strayed from YOUR POWER.
Forgive me.
Reveal my sin.
Help me name it.
Cleanse me Oh Lord.
I know I am weak.
Fill up my being with YOUR Holy Spirit again.
Give me discernment when crisis crashes in on me.
When my battles come, I will not be alone.
I must purpose daily to live from a clean heart.
Then I can praise YOU, the God who intervenes.
I must know the Word of God so I can pray it.
I choose to put on the armor of God; the breastplate of righteousness, the helmet of salvation, the belt of Truth, my feet clad in the Gospel of peace, praying in the power of the Holy Spirit, taking of the shield of Faith and the sword of the Spirit which is God's Word.
As YOUR child the Blood of Jesus is my covering of protection.

I will resist all darkness and schemes of the enemy of my soul to thwart my life,
Resisting in prayer in the authority of Jesus' Name.
Released, I will purpose to pray, live and overcome.
For I know my Redeemer lives!

SURGING THOUGHTS

Why is a clean heart necessary?

Do you believe there is an adversary who prowls around as a lion, a tempter, and a ruler of darkness who seeks to destroy?

Have you ever prayed the scripture known as the "armor of God" found in Ephesians 6: 10-18?

Do you have some battle verses to pray when you experience the darkness of the oppressor?

Here are some suggestions:

Psalm 27:13-14
Psalm 103: 8-14
Psalm 138: 7-8,
Zephaniah 3:16-17
II Corinthians 9:8
I John 1:9

Oh Thou my God, stand by me against the world

Martin Luther

Chapter Ten

PRAYER TO GALVANIZE

Surging prayer *gathers*.

The life of Jesus gathered.
"Prayer is the heart of spiritual experience…a life lived in communion and dependence upon Jesus." (1)
He knew we would need to come together to pray for each other.
He patterned this with his disciples.
Prayer was integral to Him.
"The evidence is clear. Jesus' strength of ministry and depth of compassion was both directly related to the consistency and vitality of his personal prayer life." (2)
It was the habit of His life to seek His Father.
He modeled a praying life.
It was paramount.

Very early in the morning, while it was still dark, Jesus got up, left the house and went to a solitary place, where he prayed (3)

He knew we must learn the personal discipline of prayer.
There was more.
Jesus was a gatherer.
He gathered twelve men, investing Himself, guiding them into Truth, and teaching them to pray.
Prayer is an avenue of community.
A prayer gathering reaches across races, nations, and prejudices and injustices becoming a mighty voice unto God breaking down barriers, bringing hope, encouragement and healing.
God instructs us to *gather*.

He who is not with me is against me and he who does not gather with me scatters. (4)

To gather or to scatter,
What will it be?
Praying together bonds a people who will seek the heart of God, uniting as one before the One True God, creating a force of prayer.
Scripture gives us a picture of such a gathering.
In the fourth Chapter of Mark, members of the Sanhedrin, a governing body of authority, are monitoring Peter and John.
They were being watched.
Peter and John were witnessing, teaching the people, proclaiming Jesus.
A large audience of 5,000 assembled, listened and believed.
Guided by impassioned servants, a crowd became galvanized.
To galvanize is to "to arouse to awareness, to stir, to spur to action."
This flow of surging faith landed them both in jail.
The next day they were brought in and questioned.
A man had been healed.
Peter began to articulate once again the impact of Jesus' life, the authority of His Name, His influence.
The council members were amazed at the knowledge and courage of Peter and John.
Described as unschooled, ordinary men, *they took note that they these men had been with Jesus.* (5)
Indeed they had.
The healed man was not present but he had been healed.
The members of the council huddled together to figure out what to do about Peter and John.
This miracle had to be squelched, contained.
To forbid them to speak further was the course of action decided.
Peter and John refused.

We cannot help speaking about what we have seen and heard. (6)

People noted their courageous stance and began to praise God openly.
Frustrated accusers unable to stop this display were compelled to let them go.
The favor of God was resting in power upon Peter and John and returning to their own people, they reported all that the chief priests and elders had said.
When their own people heard this, *they raised their voices together in prayer to God, 'Sovereign Lord, you made the heaven and the earth and the sea and everything in them…now Lord consider their threats and enable your servants to speak your word with great boldness… through the name of your holy servant*

Jesus.' (7)

What were they calling for?

"The apostles were unjustly arrested, imprisoned, and threatened...they didn't call for a protest. They didn't initiate a letter-writing campaign. They didn't use their political clout. Instead they called a prayer meeting." (8)

They needed a prayer meeting.

And the place was shaken.

A surging force was galvanized.

What happens when people pray together?

We become unified and the Kingdom Of God is expanded.

This would be the summons of God for future believers, to assemble, to convene, to pray with one another for one another

What is the significance of this?

Early Christians met regularly for prayer together.

They all met together continually for prayer.... (9)

So must we.

This is the plan for empowering us to be a magnetic presence for God in this world.

Author Rick Warren coined the phrase, "better, together."

And we are.

Our faith is corporate, many sided, multi dimensioned and each one of us brings some aspect of it to the prayer gathering.

When we surge together in prayer, how the heart of God must overflow.

He desires that we weave our hearts together in prayer.

Life is bigger than our corner.

His name is Brennan Hawkins.

On a camping trip with the Boy Scouts in Utah, he became separated from the group.

The last time Brennan was seen, he was climbing a wall.

A search began.

So did the anguish.

People came from all over the country to give their time, to aid.

His father would go out in the field daily, seeking.

His mother would work with the volunteers at the "headquarters."

Intense, exhausted, determined were those who came.

And prayer began to rise.

The media had his face on every news broadcast daily.
Our hearts were moved to enter the crisis,
Urged to pray.
We witnessed the massive effort.
We were drawn into the pain
We were not physically on site but we were an army crying out to God for this young boy's life.
Thousands were drawn to pray and so collectively we were one voice unto God even though we were in different places.
Four days later, a rescue worker stumbled upon Brennan who was standing, looking waiting.
He had had no water or food for four days, but was described as miraculously in good condition.
What elation exploded.
What emotion spilled over as tears of gratitude and relief flowed.
What joy and thanksgiving did his parents express.
How did this happen?
His mother said, "The heavens were not closed. God answers prayer...."
He does.
Brennan, age eleven returned to his home in a suburb called Bountiful.
God's bounty for him was galvanized through prayer
And we are a line of defense.

Prayer equips others to serve.

Men and women serving in a time of war need a deliberate covering of prayer over them.
They need the community of prayer.
From the words of our son, Chaplain Carey Cash, as he served with his battalion in the spring of 2003;
"There in the Mojave Desert night we worshiped God, sang hymns of faith, shared prayer requests, and allowed the Lord to speak to us from His Word. My sermon was brief, but considering the ominous state of the world and where we might find ourselves in the months to come, I thought its theme was fitting: Fear Not.
My text was II Timothy 1:7 *'For God has not given us a spirit of fear, but of power and love and a sound mind.'* (10)
Prayer disarms fear, reminding us of the Love of God and then we can think with clarity, soundness of mind, and reassurance that He is near.
So the community of faith must continue to gather to pray for those in

harm's way.

Around the world our voices are raised for sons and daughters, friends and strangers who are serving the nations in the armed forces in danger.

God moves collectively in this call.

He gathers us to pray.

Words from our daughter-in-law Charity, Carey's wife:

"…This is a faith shaking and hopefully a building time for many people. I can't imagine not knowing the Lord. He is all I have to cling to…let all the guys know that literally thousands and thousands of people are praying for them." (11)

I am one of them.

I will always be one of them.

Will you?

God calls us to be one of them.

Prayer shapes the future.

Praying for my children was the ground breaking work for a praying life.

Years spent alone with a husband going to sea gave me time, time to pray.

I leaned into God's Word and developed a hunger to know it.

Bible classes followed, life experience, gatherings with women seemed to be sign posts pointing to path leading me to affirm women.

I had a background in communication and music.

I was being compelled to reach out.

From time to time I would speak to women's groups on a variety of issues.

My friend Peggy was always in the audience as a support whether it was Navy wives, a Bible study group or church banquet.

After showing up for on several occasions she asked me a pointed question; "Do you have any one who prays for you when you speak?"

I smiled and said, "Yes, my mother and Roy."

She laughed and said, "**You** are going to need a lot of prayer."

She was right.

She was God's handmaiden ready to organize a prayer group that would serve as a covering over the ministry that God was orchestrating.

She prayed for direction in selecting women who would be asked to participate.

One by one they came.

I was undone, humbled

The security of a prayer covering,

I longed for it.

I just couldn't believe God would tap someone to do it.

He did.

Meeting once a month at Peggy's home, we would have from three to ten women.

I would share the details for the upcoming speaking commitment coupled with my thoughts gleaned by intuition.

Then they prayed.

After I had spoken at the event, I would write in a journal and when we met again, I would relate to them how God answered their prayers.

It was exciting.

Their prayer fueled my faith, opened my heart to boldness.

We were woven together in friendship, love, and purpose.

There would be tears, laughter, hugs, and celebration as we gathered.

Relationships bloomed.

Sharing our lives in community allowed His Love to be exuberantly communicated in ministry.

God was in our midst.

These journals were the inspiration for my first book, *Windows of Assurance*.

Prayer invests.

Years later, when I began to cross the nation, traveling overseas to speak, I looked back upon that precious cluster of "Little Women" who were mighty in prayer.

I was awed at what God did with a handful of homemakers who had praying lives.

It was the launching of my ministry with women.

All that I do is founded in prayer.

People need praying lives.

One day I began to ponder how a prayer effort could reach around the world.

If many could pray for someone, what would happen?

I wondered how I could enlarge the scope of reaching out in prayer.

God wants to stretch us.

Early one morning I prayed,

Lord, show me how to follow through when I say I will pray…show me how to do this.

I began to think about the computer and how to utilize it for prayer.

On my web site and through e-mail, I would receive requests to pray.

I wanted to be faithful.

One morning it occurred to me that I should stop right then and voice a prayer or better yet write a prayer and then share that prayer with my base of about 200 people.

They in turn would share it with their list of praying friends.

Before I could comprehend it, there was an assembling internationally of folks who were praying for the needs of others.

This became a pattern.

I would write a prayer and send it out over the Internet.

There is great satisfaction in participating in prayer this way.

It can be read over and over again.

Someone has prayed.

The prayer is before them.

It becomes a prayer of agreement as one voice but many are praying.

Then the idea came to me to pray this way for my pastor, worship leader, and some other staff on a systematic, consistent basis.

I prayed again.

Lord, show me how to do this.

He did.

Once a week, I go to God's Word and ask Him to guide me to write a prayer for these who lead, who need refreshment, courage, stamina and the blessing of God.

Would I have time to do this?

Will you?

Make it a prayer request unto Him.

All our time is in His Hands.

And He has made the time for me to do this.

He makes a way, for prayer is always on His heart.

There is a small group of women in my city who pray me through writing and speaking.

There is an inner circle of women scattered throughout the country who pray me through all I do.

There is a Bible class of believers in my church who encircle Roy and me with love and acceptance, praying us through our daily lives.

Community works.

This little assembly of the faithful has prayed through many trials for others; a successful liver transplant for a five-year old, job losses, cancer, depression, emotional pain, broken children, spiritual struggle, death.

We do life together,

And we are not done.

To be a part of such a circle of faith, a gathering of pilgrims is to have another family.

God uses circumstance to gather us.
Prayer galvanizes faith, moving it forward.

> There are only two ways to live your life.
> One is though nothing is a miracle.
> The other is as though everything is a miracle.
> Albert Einstein

It is.
God calls us to gather, cooperating in the miraculous, surging in prayer like the force of a mighty river.
"Let the river run through us and empty in our hearts," (12)

There is a time for everything and a season for every activity under the heaven… a time to scatter…a time to gather…. (13)

We gather together to ask the Lord's blessing,
He chastens and hastens His Will to make known,
The wicked oppressing now ceases from distressing,
Sing praises to His Name,
He forgets not His own.

It's time to gather, gather to pray.
Galvanized we will surge in prayer becoming a force of faith in this world.

PRAYER FLOW

Ever-Vigilant Father;
We are one in YOU.
Unite us to pray as brothers and sisters.
YOUR HAND directs praying hearts.
How many times have I refused to come together for anything?
Solo is not your plan.
Together is.
Forgive me.
Prompt me.
Use me.
We are better, together.
YOU are calling us daily to intercede.

Stir us to respond.
Gather us in Jesus' Name to remember His example and to breathe hope
for another.
Some are losing ground.
Some are leaning into the wind.
Some love only themselves.
Grow our love for our neighbor.
Prayer is God's good gift.
Jesus, we come, In YOUR NAME together.

SURGING THOUGHTS

Why do I reject being a part of a group?

Is it possible that praying together with others makes a difference?

How does God want to enlarge my vision of prayer?

Teach me to breathe deeply in faith

Soren Kierkguaard

Chapter Eleven

PRAYER TO ENCOUNTER

Surging prayer engages.

One verb definition of engage is to "interconnect; to bring into operation...
activate, energize, join, switch on."
We pray to encounter, "to happen upon, come across, meet up with, run
into, fall in with, face, experience" God.
"Encountering" prayer is surging prayer.
Experiencing God is the goal.
Broken people need a **pray-er** – one who will intercede.
Our God calls us do the bidding.
He is grieved when no one does.

*The Lord saw...there was no justice and was astonished that there was no one
to intercede.* (1)

He wondered that there was no intercessor. (2)

...No one would do a thing about it. (3)

He couldn't believe what he saw: not a soul around to correct this awful situation.
(4)

God sorrows over the void in prayer.
If we are to clear the road of rocks and to lift up the lowly, we must pray
for encounters with God.
This is a work of entering into His heart for people

Teach me your way, O Lord and I will walk in your truth. (5)

Why would He limit Himself to people like us?
Does He need us or does He choose to use us?

"Very simply, He could not grant us freedom to choose if He were free to interfere. Therefore in some things, He must wait until our spirits are broken and given to Him. This seems to be a great secret of intercessory prayer. When God finds people who are broken enough to spend themselves in prayer for the sake of others, it releases Him to do what He couldn't do until He found those broken people." (6)

Jesus said *this is my body which is broken for you.*(7)

His life was broken for us and our brokenness gives us a heart to pray for others.

A broken heart knows the ache of another.

"Likewise in intercessory prayer… when we are broken enough in spirit, When we care more about the beloved than ourselves, it frees God to do what He could not do because of His own self-limitation. Until then…we are not seeking to free God to do what *we* want Him to do, but what *He* wants us to do" (8)

He calls us to impact others through prayer.

Prayer engages the heart.

God encounters the life.

When we believe this, we will with gladness embrace His perspective, seeing with eyes of love and compassion.

He uses our brokenness.

I am glad it can be used.

It was a steamy July day at a pancake house in Biloxi, Mississippi.

We were down there for a summertime break on the coast.

My husband, Roy, and I were seated at a small table and immediately began to look at the menu. Within minutes, I was keenly aware that a family was being seated next to us. There appeared to be a father, a boy about ten years old and a girl about eight. They were on one side of the table. Across from them were two teenaged girls and a lady on the end. I could only see one of the teens because she was seated at he end across from me. The restaurant was overflowing with folks, a very busy Saturday.

Roy and I ordered our food and then he left to go to the car to get a map. In the moments that followed I was swept up into a heart wrenching empathy for these children as a lack of relationship was displayed at the table.

I was quickened to pray.

This was a family having a meal, attempting to feign a normalcy they did not have. The father, who was perhaps in his early forties with thinning dark unruly hair, was unkempt and demanding in his demeanor. He wore an angry, suspicious scowl upon his face, barking and then screaming at the children.

He called attention to himself.

No one at the table spoke freely.

I sensed abuse as I looked at their tense faces.

The teenager closest to me looked like someone marking her time, preparing an exit strategy. She was dressed in jeans, a white tee shirt. Her long earthy brown hair hung limp upon her shoulders framing her face with an expression of glazed-over despondency.

This was not a new scene for her.

She had played it out many times.

On every finger of her hands was a collection of silver rings of all kinds and shapes. She played with the rings, twisting them, looking down as the father gruffly told all of them what they could order.

His speech was rudely loud.

Money was the issue.

It was the little girl's child-like expression that captured mine.

She glanced up and appeared to question him.

Pouncing upon her words, he said, "Shut up!"

She, being a child, instinctively began to play with the bottles of pancake syrup asking every one at the table which kind they would like – like a child planning a tea party.

Spontaneously she lovingly reached to stroke his hair, to touch him as if to make up a bit and at that moment he grabbed her hand and railed on her, "I told you, one more thing and I am taking you out of here."

Such fury at a child's attempt to connect, to be intimate.

She did not cry or tear up, just quietly faded into her world of diversion by picking up a napkin folding it different ways.

I fought back hot tears for her rejection.

Roy finally walked up and I whispered to him what I had observed.

A kind gray-haired matron came to serve the food to them. It was mostly bread, biscuits and pancakes, no meat or eggs.

They began to wolf the food down ravenously as if starved.

Then I heard this dear little girl with soft brown chestnut hair and a cautious look say, "S'cuse me ma'am, how much does a bowl of gravy cost?"

That did it.

Roy and I immediately caught each other's eyes and knew we would be paying for this meal anonymously.

We motioned to the sympathetic waitress and explained what we wanted to do, asking her to give us the bill and to explain to them that someone had paid it.

She smiled and said, "That'd be real good. They need it I think."

I said, "Yes, I know they do."

Then she broadened her smile and said, "God will bless you, ma'am. It always comes back."

It had.

I could barely swallow.

I was so burdened for this family, for the children.

They needed an encounter with God.

But right now they were hungry.

The family finished their meal and left the restaurant. The waitress came to Roy and me and told us they were thrilled about their good fortune.

A bill had been paid.

Freely given,

Freely received.

"Thank you, Lord. O, God, make a way for this family today. Feed them, love them, free them because of Jesus."

We encounter God through prayer.

He engages the heart.

Gravy and God's Love do go together.

I shall never forget the constraining immediacy to respond.

We are to be eyes and ears on this faith journey, to move with God as He moves us along.

Brokenness moves us to pray.

Persistence is a work of the will.

It brings definition to our character.

There was a woman, a widow in the Bible that kept harassing a judge.

She felt she had been wronged and would not let go of the matter but continued to seek justice day after day.

The judge refused.

She kept coming.

Finally he said to himself, 'even though I don't fear God or care about men yet because this widow keeps bothering me, I will see that she gets justice so that she won't eventually wear me out with her coming.' (9)

Think about it.

If an insensitive, callous judge will submit to a persistent widow, what will a gracious and good God do for the one who persists in prayer?

Here's what He will do.

Will not God bring about justice for these chosen ones, who cry out to him day and night? Will he keep putting them off? I tell you he will see that they get justice.... (10)

God allows us to partner with Him, to intercept in prayer those He places before us along the way in this faith journey.

Enter Moses, a tongue-tied Hebrew leader who not only stutters but actually debates with God on Mount Sinai. He goes there to receive the Ten Commandments and while he is away his own "stiff-necked people" fashion an idol out of gold.
God becomes angry.

Leave me alone so that my anger may burn against them.... (11)

Moses intercepts God.

He encountered the living God. *Moses sought the favor of the Lord his God... O Lord... why should your anger burn against your people whom you brought out of Egypt with great power and a mighty hand...Turn from your fierce anger; relent and do not bring disaster on your people.* (12)

God heard his prayer.

The Lord relented and did not bring on his people the disaster he had threatened. (13)
The God of the Universe was moved to change His mind by one faithful, obedient praying man.
Our God listens when His people call out to Him.
Another riveting encounter of such consequence is also recorded for us in the Bible.
It bears a timely scrutiny.

Her name is Esther.
There is fascination surrounding the story of Esther.
Beautiful indeed, virtuous Esther was brought into the palace of King Xerxes.
Commissioners in every province were appointed to assist in the *search for beautiful young virgins for the king.* (14)
Why?
Because Vashti the queen was going to be replaced.

She had messed up.
Lovely in appearance as well, Vashti had been summoned to an important celebration in which the King wanted to display her beauty.
He sent for her.
She refused.

When the attendants delivered the king's command Queen Vashti refused. (15)

Such a demonstration of insolence was not acceptable to a king.
Hegei, the king's eunuch was chosen to be in charge of overseeing the search for a new queen.
Why?
The women would be safe with him.
Who was Esther?
She was an orphaned Jew whose adopted father was Mordecai.
He was in fact her cousin and her other name was Hadassah. (16)
When her parents died he stepped into the role as father.
No one knew she was a Jew.
Mordecai had forbidden her to reveal it.
Every day Hegei watched Esther.
Every day Mordecai watched him.

Every day he (Mordecai) walked back and forth near the courtyard of the harem to find out how Esther was and what was happening to her. (17)

Esther easily won the favor of Hegei.
Supervised beauty treatments began for twelve months: *six months with oil of myrrh and six months with perfume* and cosmetis. (18)
Special food.
Seven maids to assist her,
The best place in the harem.
The time came for her to appear before the king and she won his approval.
Esther was made queen and a banquet was given in her honor.
God was actively involved in this scenario for He was preparing Esther for an encounter that would alter the history of a nation
Mordecai, a man of integrity, uncovered a plot to assassinate Xerxes.
He disclosed this to Esther who exposed it to the king.
The instigators met their just demise.
She had beauty plus loyalty.

Now Haman enters the foray, a man with a lust for adulation and position.

Erroneously honored by the king, he decides that all others should bow down to him.

Mordecai would not submit.

The enraged Haman then purposed to destroy not only him but also his people, the Jews.

Going to the king, Haman identifies the Jews as the group who would not adhere to the customs of the king.

He follows through with this charge convincing Xerxes to issue an edict to destroy them.

An ominous horror descends upon the Jewish people accompanied by mourning, fasting, weeping, wailing, sackcloth and ashes.

A cry unto a God who intervenes.

A cry accompanied by fasting, a choice to "abstain from food as a religious discipline."

The Jewish people knew that the intervention of a Holy God in dire situations would require fasting, a focused withdrawal from food in order to focus on breakthrough in prayer.

The best defense is a decisive spiritual offense.

Jesus said, **When** (not if) you fast...your father who sees what is done in secret, will reward you. (19)

Fasting was a part of the praying life of the Jews.

Esther finds out about the decree, seeks Mordecai for direction and he admonishes her to go before the king, to plead for the Jewish people.

To appear in the inner court before Xerxes the king, unannounced was an offense punishable by death.

One exception remained.

If the king extended the golden scepter, the life of the individual was spared.

This is what Esther did:

Go gather together all the Jews who are in Susa to fast for me. Do not eat or drink for three days, night or day. I and my maids will fast as you do. When this is done, I will go to the king, even though it is against the law. If I perish, I perish. (20)

She did not perish.

Neither did her nation.

What had Esther learned in the months of preparation to be queen?

She knew brokenness for she was an orphan.

She was obedient to Godly authority because she received instruction respectfully from Mordecai.

She succumbed to the daily ritual of a prescribed regime of beauty treatments for a year.

She learned to be persistent for there were high expectations required.

When the encounter came to stand for justice, it was delivered in prayer and fasting.

Queens and common folks all need intercession.

Sometimes we will need to fast and pray.

> *Guard the fortress*
> *Watch the road*
> *Brace yourselves*
> *Marshall all your strength*
> Nahum 2:1

Responsible faith will intercede in prayer.

"God uses our offerings – our meager check written to help feed the hungry, our quiet smile of encouragement, and no less our praying – to transfigure the world and unfold unimaginable purposes. Jesus tells us not only to ask, seek, and knock, but he says that if we do, we will receive, we will find, and a door will open. This points not only to a promise of what *can* happen; it suggests what may *not* happen if we ignore the invitation. The world does not bow to an impersonal fate. God is on the move, and he enlists us in his kingdom advance." (21)

Surging prayer encounters God so that He can engage hearts that need hope.

Let's sing a prayer from this great musical refrain:

Have faith in God when your pathway is lonely
He sees and knows all the way you have trod.
Never alone are the least of His children.
Have faith in God.
Have faith in God.
Have faith in God, He's on His throne;
Have faith in God, He watches o'er His own;
He cannot fail, He must prevail;
Have faith in God,
Have faith in God.

In faith we prevail in prayer and touch heaven for another.
Sometimes it is the course of a nation.
Sometimes it's a meal.
Life for someone changes because we prayed.

PRAYER FLOW

Faithful Father;
Give me a heart to hear and ears that will listen to the world around me.
Stir me to respond to YOUR call of encounter.
Open someone's life today to the Love of a Savior.
Engage them.
Someone somewhere intercepted me long ago.
I cannot do less.
I shall respond.
Keep me at it, Lord,
In Jesus' Name

SURGING THOUGHTS

Have you ever been in a public place and been urged to stop and pray for someone?

Have you ever done a random act of kindness on the spot?

Have you thanked God today for His faithfulness?

Keep us Lord awake in the duty of our calling.

John Donne

A PURPOSED DILIGENCE

From strength to strength, go on!
Wrestle and fight and pray
Tread all the powers of darkness down,
And win the well-fought day!

Charles Wesley

Chapter Twelve
PRAYING A DESTINY

Surging prayer hugs the world.

God cares about the nations.
Passionately.
I can go to a foreign country through prayer.
I did.
In the writing of this book, I have been to Tanzania and to Spain regularly.
These are the people I have met:

Precious Laura Lee is a missionary to Tanzania and it has been my privilege to send God's Love and encouragement to her in prayer.
She is serving a two-year assignment as a journeyman with an International Mission Board in Dar es Saalam. Laura Lee's aunt Cathy, a lovely friend of mine e-mailed me asking me to pray for her niece.
I knew immediately I was to do so.
These are her words as she describes the call of God upon her life:
"God has been working in my heart and life...He planted seeds of his call on a mission trip to Brazil and began to confirm my call in the summer of 2003... I began to pray over people groups, and areas of the world, lifting up God's purposes in each place...seeking to discern where He might want me to serve, praying in response to needs...praise, warfare...as I began to take ownership and responsibility for these people groups, fighting for them in prayer, God developed my heart for the nations in a fresh, specific, living and urgent way."

Declare His Glory among the nations. (1)

She has.

Laura's calling was birthed and sustained through prayer.

As we have prayed for her she tells us what God did. "Through those prayers, dorm rooms have swung open wide for me to build relationships and usher in the truth as well as guidance and equipping for many girls in their walk with the Lord. I have become accustomed to breathing prayers wherever I am, whether in catching a crowded mini bus and praying for those on either side of me, or prayer walking the campus, sitting with my neighbors, praying prayers they cannot hear and won't know about but God is hearing. I am able to be an advocate for these people, remembering them before God, asking for an out pouring of His Spirit as a loving father who wants His children to be in His arms, abiding with Him and growing strong… seeking to plant *'oaks of righteousness, a planting of the Lord.'*" (2)

A praying life gives.

These words shape the beginning of her experience on campus in Dar es Saalam:
"As I was sitting and praying at one of the stone tables on campus in respite from the heat under the palm trees, I experienced one of the great wonders of Tanzania…the majority of the students have no qualms plopping down next to a perfect stranger and making themselves at home. I knew God had just the right place for me. Talk about a people group I was made for!"
When relationships begin, prayer begins to rise.
"Please pray God will give me a close national friend."
He did.
The months that unfolded were bathed in prayer for break throughs, drinking water, safety, and spiritual growth, time to renew, time to study and prepare Bible studies.
I went in prayer to the Maasai village of Arusha with Laura Lee and Neema as they used the tool of Bible *storying* the Good News of the Gospel.
When a story is told, it gathers people.
She presented a Maasai Bible to Neema's family.
Laura Lee describes Bible *storying* for the first time with her neighbor kids on their front stoop. "Imagine ten kids with no idea of personal space chiming in on my simple account of Genesis I, then acting out the story of creation! I told the story in Kiswahili with lots of help from a Swahili Bible storybook and help from the kids. As I left, they told me to come back and tell them more stories every day!"
Her neighborhood children were a personal delight.
Her stories spilled over and her course was constantly altered through praying for others. After pouring out her energies, semester after semester,

students would graduate from the university and then it was time to begin again with new ones.

Always ready with inspiration, Laura Lee imparted vision.

Listen to her words forged from the Word of God:

"The Lord will go forth like a warrior. He will rouse His zeal like a man of war."

"In the movie, *Braveheart*, Mel Gibson gallops through the lines of his fellow fighting men, spurring them on to courageous battle. His passion and his presence inspired all those fighting beside him. Have you ever thought about God as a warrior? Isaiah 42 paints a beautiful picture of the zeal God has for His own. He doesn't stand on the sidelines as a helpless and feeble observer hoping someone will remember His name, but rather charges ahead, raising a war cry and prevailing against His enemies. Like a warrior riding with His Company in battle, I see him rousing zeal in His soldiers as He joins them in the fight and strengthens their confidence in a sure victory."

This is just one account of God's call upon her life.

Laura Lee is no shrinking violet but an empowered, young woman of destiny. Her photographs present a willowy, fair, sensitive face framed by long sun kissed hair, like an opening sunflower reaching up to the Son of God. Bearing a gentle, compassionate countenance with an easy smile, Laura Lee seems to be comfortable with people. Her natural prettiness is refreshing, unorchestrated. Equipped to be in this land, she reveals how she prays:

"I have been praying that God would raise up an army of bold proclaimers of His name from among the university students of Dar es Salaam. I want to make disciples who are not afraid to boldly speak the name of Christ who have confidence in their victory by His Grace. As the praises of His people spread from nation to nation all over the earth, His glory is made great."

I joined her in praise and petition.

Precious and Holy God,
I thank You for Your diligent servant who can articulate the need, know the enemy, raise up a standard and pursue it with vigor and commitment.
Hear our prayer for her tonight…Oh Lord, we are coming into agreement in asking for a body of bold proclaimers in Jesus from the student body of Dar es Salaam. Give each one God ordained discernment, knowledge of the Word, a praying life and assurance in the victory of Jesus. Bring questioning, seeking students across Laura Lee's path that are watching the flow of her faith and wondering what she has that they do not. Birth a desire in each new believer to see the completion

of true faith in the Living God in his or her village. Call them into prayer, bible study, seeking Your Holy Spirit daily so they will be found ready and able. Give them a vision of Your Glory and establish their purpose in YOU....

I prayed for Adela, Doreen, Linda, Ilumba, Ruth, Sanura and Zainab and many others.
And God answered those prayers.

> *Know that the Lord has set apart the godly for Himself.*
> *The Lord will hear when I call to him.*(3)

What a work God is raising up in Tanzania through the efforts of Laura Lee who is there reaching nationals who will in turn reach their own for Christ.
With joy I have been delighted to come alongside of her in prayer.
A nation is being reached with the Love of God and we are being changed as we pray for other lands.

But there was more.
There was Elliot, a captivatingly handsome young man with inquisitive brown eyes, dark curly hair and an infectious smile.
While attending Georgia Tech as a student, Elliott was one of twelve involved with the Georgia Tech Christian Campus Fellowship. They banded together as a team and were called to the area of Salamanca, Spain for seventeen weeks.
Since I have known his parents Rob and Margrett and his grandparents, Annette and Whitey for many years, I was drawn with affection to be a part of his prayer covering.
His e-mails were chocked full of adventure.
The team began to pray for a house to rent so that students could be invited to come and have meals, do Bible study, grow fellowship and build community. Would you believe that the house God chose for them had a main room three levels underground? How perfectly situated was this arrangement. There was space and noise containment as students would come and go.
The house that was to be a house of prayer, refuge and spiritual awakening became an answer to prayer. Much paperwork was required for an American leasing Spanish property, which involved taxes and an acceptable rental agreement.
They prayed.
God met the need abundantly.

Elliot wrote, "This whole city is one big opportunity for God to do something amazing. We are here to meet students, become their friends and then show them Christ's love. We meet outside of the main library on the campus twice a day to hand out free coffee and pastries to the students taking finals. The students are taken aback that we would want to give something for free. We give them the opportunity to sign up with us – to be apart of *intercambios* (times to meet one on one, helping each other with our respective languages, making friends). As we prayed about this, about 70 agreed to meet with us."

This endeavor would be the beginning of the team's purpose for coming to Spain, to establish a campus ministry for the university students.

And it did begin.

Later as they had retreats, bus excursions to Andalucia and Seville, *seeking* relationships *did* begin to form. He describes a conversation with a Spanish girl who was being drawn to an intercambio group. He heard her speaking with another team member in Spanish, and then she said in English, "I don't believe in anything, not in God or anyone else. I believe in myself."

He reacted.

She saw Elliot's response to her statements and asked him if he felt sad.

He said, "I guess I am sad."

To which she replied, "Why are you sad?"

"I am sad that you don't believe in anything."

She continued, "Don't be sad for me, I'm fine."

He would not let go.

"No, really I am sad that you don't…believe in God."

Elliot had already had discussions on a variety of topics before this one with her and now he knew "God was working in her life…allowing *him* to watch it unfold."

Reflectively she answered, "Maybe you can help me believe in something."

He did.

On a trip to Grenada, Elliot mentions meeting with another girl there who "couldn't stop talking about how much God had changed her life. It encouraged our whole team."

One girl on a search for God.

One girl who had found Him.

Called to pray through this exciting time in Spain, anticipating God, I came:

Beloved Father:
It is wonderful to hear and sense expectancy in Elliot's voice about his mission

with the Spanish people.
We believe you will provide the house they need which will be a refuge for the
team as well as a place of ministry in prayer and Bible study.
Identify it soon.
We ask that YOU choose the encounters Elliot is to have – the intercambios/
comedor experiences. Conversations with young people on campus armed with
coffee and pastries are a great combination for prepared hearts dressed in the full
armor of God daily. Choose his way. Chart his course. Guard his heart. Keep
him clean and filled with Your Spirit. This team will be making a difference in
Your Kingdom.
Orchestrate a time of retreat regularly for purity, clarity and a deepening
relationship with YOU. It's all about people, Lord, friendship in Christ Jesus for
the Kingdom.

Many wonderful answers came from my visit to Spain in prayer for Elliot.
He referred to this time as an opportunity for "being Jesus" to those
students and he says now that he is back at school, "the experience in
Spain reminds me how life can be when we place total faith in Him."

What a privilege to pray for those serving in foreign lands.

"God has given us prayer because Jesus has given us a mission. God's
pleasure in the prayers of his people is proportionate to his passion for the
world...we are on this earth to press back the forces of darkness and we are
given access to Headquarters by prayer in order to advance this cause." (4)
We change the world through prayer.

Paul the apostle knew this truth and asked for it in the scripture.
Pray also for me, that utterance may be given me in opening my mouth boldly to
proclaim the mystery of the gospel. (5)
Pray also that God may open a door for the Word, to declare the mystery of
Christ. (6)
Finally, brothers, pray for us, that the Word of the Lord may be glorified. (7)

When I began this book, I knew that writing about prayer would be a
challenging extension of my own praying.
It has.
There has been much to pray about as I have written.
Illnesses, calamities, uncertainties and pressures have been my constant
companions.

But in whatever is written, I want to experience God.

I have.

In my research for this book, it was fascinating to note that the imminent scholar C. S. Lewis whose writings have fed the faith of generations of seekers, never wrote a book on prayer.

He wanted to do so but it never happened.

"For some time Jack [C.S. Lewis] had wanted to write a book on prayer, but it had not worked out. He made an attempt but it faltered…He abandoned the work until early in 1963, when the idea came to him to write about prayer in an imaginary series of letters to a friend. It was to be called *Letters to Malcolm*." (8)

Writing on prayer is a test in prayer.

A lot can happen to keep you from it.

As I walked along the shoreline of the Alabama Gulf coast one sparkling August morning, I was praying about how to bring love and resolution to a situation.

God was preparing me to write about prayer

It was the first light of daybreak, luminous with shades of ripened apricot interlaced with faint aqua glints highlighting the warm golden rays of sunlight softly emerging. This picture of the sky was very much like a vast seashell opening up to reveal its incandescent lining of mother of pearl.

All color seems to layer itself hue upon hue in mother of pearl.

The striking effect was a translucent, glowing heaven above me.

Shades of sea green waves were lapping gently at my feet as I walked and prayed.

"Show me Lord, what YOU want me to see and learn, what YOU want me to do."

As my gaze fell across the stretch of cushioned, bleached sand, my eye was immediately drawn to an elaborately detailed sand castle.

It had wings and spires, doors and windows.

I marveled at the artistry.

Shaped by hand, dug in sand but placed perilously close to the water's edge,

It was a fragile serendipity for a brief moment.

In a flash the tide would come and it would be swept away.

Momentary beauty…

I continued to walk and abruptly collided with a single, abandoned, blue tennis shoe left on the beach.

Its mate was elsewhere

One shoe won't take you anywhere.

Direction....
Before I returned to the condominium, I stumbled upon a small silver coated fish that had washed upon the shore, gasping, a fish out of water trying to live.
Still alive, all it needed was to be picked up by somebody and thrown back into water
And I did.
Timing...

What was I to learn from these objects God put in my path?

What am I building that's lasting?

Where am I going?

How can I live?

Significance, focus, life.

A praying life makes a difference.
It has all of these dimensions and more.

In the writing of this book I have asked several friends this question.

What does prayer mean to you?

Judy said, "Prayer is time with God, rolling around in the love of His Heart."
Anne added, "Prayer is the awesome privilege of...sitting and talking to my Abba Father."
Denise exclaimed, "Prayer is my opportunity to breathe praise to my Father...my Everything."
Joyce responded with, "Prayer is my sharing with God things that are happening in my life that I'm not able to share with others."
Stephanie declared, "I live by prayer because it is the only way to live the life God has chosen for me...open communication with Him alone."

Then I asked why do you pray for others?

"To receive His Love for others and to stand with Him sharing His

Love...."
"He has put a love for others in my heart – therefore I pray."
"His love compels me."
"I have desperately needed prayer myself so I must respond."
"Some people don't have the faith to trust God to ...care for the needs in their life."

Who is this that rises...like rivers of surging waters? (9)

It's you and me.
It's a praying life.
You see we do have a story to tell to the nations, a song to sing, a praying life to offer.
Will you accept the call to pray, to surge in prayer for someone here or in another land?
It is a transforming call to an overcoming life.
We overcome through prayer.
Every time.
Someone's destiny depends upon it.

He leadeth me, O blessed thought,
O words with heavenly comfort fraught.
Whate'er I do, where'er I be
Still 'tis God's hand that leadeth me.

He will lead us to pray.

Will prayer become an internal silent dialogue between you and your Maker, a sure compass, a work of eternity, bringing beauty to your soul, encircling all the days of your life?
It can.
It did so in the life of Amy Carmichael.

Let us join our hearts together in a prayer she prayed long ago.

God of the deeps, how near Thou art;
Here are Thy garments; sea and shore.
Beauty of all things show in part
Thee whom, unseen, we love, adore.
Thine are the good salt winds that blow;

Thine is the magic of the sea;
Glories of colour from Thee flow,
We worship Thee, we worship Thee.

God of the tempest and the calm,
God of the timeless, patient tides,
God of the water's healing balm,
And gentle sounds where stillness bides.
God of the stainless fields of blue,
God of the grandeur of the sea,
Swifter than ever spindrift flew,
Like homing birds, we fly to thee.
God of the waves that roll and swell,
And break in tossing clouds of foam.
Thy handiwork, the painted shell
For fragile life, how safe a home.
God of the great and the small,
God of the glory of the sea,
Here, in the quite evenfall,
We worship Thee, we worship Thee.
(10)

Come with me to the shores of faith.
Love God.
Hear the call.
Rise and embrace the work of prayer.
Flow, alter and surge with me for someone
Our turn will come.
Trust God.
Be ready.
He is waiting to answer.

Your face, Lord, I will seek. (11)

If you are seeking after God,
You may be sure of this:
God is seeking you much more.

Saint John of the Cross

PRAYERSURGE

My Father and My God;
I understand now.
YOU are calling me in love to pray.
YOU have people on YOUR heart today with needs.
The turbulent world I live in demands some kind of response daily.
There are terrorists, tsunami waves, earthquakes, abductions, heinous acts,
unmitigated pain to endure,
Cries for help will come.
There is incredible beauty to be experienced.
Breath taking sunsets, majestic mountains, fragrant flower gardens, exotic rain
forests, glorious rivers and mighty oceans to enjoy,
Both praise and petition will be on our lips.
But
It is prayer,
My prayer that YOU seek.
I must hear the call.
I will respond.
Nudge me.
Stir me.
Waken me.
Enable me.
Reveal
YOUR GLORY
Speak Lord, for YOUR servant is listening.
In Jesus' Love, I will surge in prayer for others.

Chapter Thirteen

SURGING PRAYER TIDES

In prayer it is better to have a heart without words than words without heart

John Bunyon

These are words I have prayed for others through overwhelming tides of circumstance.

May they encourage you and help you to pray.

PRAYER FOR A GRANDDAUGHTER'S SUCCESS

Beloved Lord,
I am praying for my precious _____
YOU are training her to be a young woman of God.
She has beauty on the outside and on the inside too.
Her heart belongs to YOU.
I ask for YOUR PRESENCE as she prepares to compete,
Dressing her heart with grace as she dresses her body.
Thank you for those special mentors who surround her with love and attention.
There is timing in all that YOU bring to us.
Some days are filled with the joy of success.
Some are not.
YOU ARE IN ALL OF THEM.
All days are good for us.
Bless my sweet granddaughter with confidence and trust in YOU,
We pray for YOUR PERFECT WILL in all the events of _____ life.
May she remember this experience as a stepping-stone in her life.
Reveal YOUR Love to her.
In Jesus' Name, I pray.

"For I know the thoughts that I think toward you, saith the LORD, thoughts of peace, and not of evil, to give you an expected end."
Jeremiah 29:11

PRAYER FOR A NEW BUSINESS

Mighty Deliverer;
Who owns the cattle on a thousand hills, we bow before YOU and come in assurance of YOUR LOVE.
YOU have blessed _____ and _____ with this business and we know competition is intense in other places but YOU are the ONE they look to for their needs.
YOU desire them to depend upon YOU alone.
I ask in Jesus' Name for a sustained increase in the customer base of their operation.
I ask in faith, belief and expectancy.
Sovereign Lord move this business into a new plateau financially in the year, 20__.
Jehovah Jireh, PROVIDER – PROVIDE!
We praise YOU for the godly witness this family is in the market place and we are asking for MORE opportunity, for their boundaries to be enlarged.
Do it again, Lord.
In Jesus' Name, I pray.

"Enlarge the place of thy tent, and let them stretch forth the curtains of thine habitations: spare not, lengthen thy cords, and strengthen thy stakes."
Isaiah 54:2

PRAYER FOR A CAREER CROSSROAD

Gracious Father;
YOU know every child, their personality, talents, ambitions, longings.
Be VERY PRESENT to _____.
We want YOUR BEST for _____.
We do not want the lure of false promise or the insatiable appetite for the world's light to blind her for the competitive struggle will never let go. She will be on to the next thing never finding the right thing established in Glory for her.
We trust in YOU.

YOU elevate or bring down what is pleasing or what is displeasing in our lives.

She has placed her life in YOUR HANDS.

Her parents have raised her to follow YOU.

So lead her *into* this endeavor or lead her *through* and let her KNOW it was YOUR doing.

Cause her to face Truth.

If YOU place her there, YOU can sustain her.

We praise YOU for YOUR WAYS not always our choice.

We rest this prayer at the foot of the CROSS whose LIGHT penetrates every area of life with illumination.

Direct this decision.

Choose for her.

In Jesus' Name, I pray.

"The LORD shall preserve thy going out and thy coming in from this time forth, and even for evermore."
Psalm 121:8

PRAYER FOR OUR TROOPS AT CHRISTMAS

Beneficent Father;

In YOUR GRACE and LOVE, I am asking tonight that YOU walk among them in this holiday season when their thoughts are of warm beds, family and home. In the daytime when readiness and risk are preparation, sing over them with YOUR BANNER of Love. Bring mail to them. Protect and bond them in camaraderie that only comes from the bond of danger and being together. Oh Lord, send legions of warring angels to flank them day and night, to walk beside armored vehicles, to stand beside them as they walk the streets of Afghanistan and Iraq. Help them to find YOUR COMPASSION in the faces of the people. We ask that believers in these nations bring the sacrifice of praise and prayer daily for their nation's liberty. Deep intercession will part the darkness and allow YOUR LIGHT to break through.

Lord, I ask on Christmas Eve, for a supernatural sense of belonging to YOU be given to them for then they will be "home" even in the desert place for YOU are HOME. My mother's heart weeps for them. YOU brought my son home and YOU carried him through as I gave him to YOU daily. Mighty Deliverer, deliver the gift of the shepherds and the Magi, a seeking heart. Allow our troops to experience Jesus this Christmas. May their hearts become the Manger and YOUR LOVE, the swaddling clothes. Bath them in awe and wonder. Give them an up close and personal Bethlehem. Yes; they are on maneuvers as the shepherds were. Give them a star to guide them.

In Jesus' Name, I pray.

"When they saw the star, they rejoiced with exceeding great joy."
Matthew 2:10

PRAYER FOR WOMEN IN PRISON

Holy God;
YOU ARE HERE.
Birth a hunger and thirst for YOU that ONLY YOU can satisfy. Let it flow to the stern unbending guards that scowled at me. Let it flow profusely the harder it gets to please the hierarchy because that will continue. Tough times and places do not take out God-strengthened, resilient, spirit-filled believing, Christian people who are behind these bars, Lord! They will persevere because they now have Resource, an eternal view of the finish line. What ministry! What character altering influence is possible! Move Holy Spirit through the prayers of these mothers for their children on the outside. What pain. What possibility there is in Christ Jesus!

These women are not numbers to YOU. Touch their souls today with fresh manna and a vision to take YOUR WORD to others who are there. Holy God, hear my prayer for these living behind walls that cannot shut out the Glory of God revealed in a life submitted to YOU. Give them liberty as they use the weapon of praise for in it flourishing hope comes. In Jesus' Name, I pray.

"Wherefore David blessed the LORD before all the congregation: and David said, Blessed be thou, LORD God of Israel our father, for ever and ever.

Thine, O LORD is the greatness, and the power, and the glory, and the victory, and the majesty: for all that is in the heaven and in the earth is thine; thine is the kingdom, O LORD, and thou art exalted as head above all.

Both riches and honour come of thee, and thou reignest over all; and in thine hand is power and might; and in thine hand it is to make great, and to give strength unto all.

Now therefore, our God, we thank thee, and praise thy glorious name."
I Chronicles 29:10-13

PRAYER FOR A CRISIS SURGERY

Mighty Creator;
A little boy needs a face.
YOU gave life to his body and designed his face. We plead for miraculous intervention of healing and mercy.
We CRY OUT for this surgery, which must be one YOU, orchestrate through human hands as they attempt to build a nose and redesign a face.
May this work be so supernatural, so completely YOURS that all will stand back in wonder and give YOU praise.
We CRY OUT for his ability to breathe, for expertise in decision making, for his doctors to know how to handle the spinal fluid leakage that threatens infection.
Give them the Potter's Hands.
Carry this mother's heart filled with anguish in YOURS.
Comfort her.
Move his earthly father to CRY OUT for this son.
Choose ministering angels to be with him who know the insecurities of children. Keep his body free from germs, touched only by sterile instruments. Choose the correct anesthesia chosen for his size, age and body make up.
Breathe Holy Spirit upon him, through, him, for him, being his very breath.
Shield him from the evil one and bring him through!
Show forth Your Glory!
How we CRY OUT for _____!
Hear our prayer and make a way for this precious life to become a MIGHTY man of God. Now thank YOU for all that YOU will do.
Many will see and come into Your Kingdom because of _____.
In Jesus' Name, I pray.

"Let my prayer come before thee: incline thine ear unto my cry."
Psalm 88:2

PRAYER FOR A PASTOR AND WORSHIP LEADER

"Let the righteous rejoice in the Lord and take refuge in Him; Let the upright in heart praise Him." Psalms 64:10

Praise the name of the Most High God!
Who delivers His own in trouble, out of trouble, through trouble.
There is no God like YOU!
Praise the Name of the Hightower we run into for REFUGE!
Who makes known to the world that HE IS ABLE!
Praise the Lord for He is Good, His mercy is everlasting!
Precious Lord we worship you in spirit and in Truth.
You have called us to pray.
We bask in YOUR PRESENCE.
We delight in YOUR LOVE.
We LIFT UP _____ today for courage and strength. Let the waves of anointing wash over him as he prepares to speak to his flock. Give him love for the critical, the slothful, and the inept. Show him Your Hands pierced for the ugly as well as the beautiful and give him some special men to undergird his every move, men of integrity and decision, uncompromising men who love YOU and not money – men of prayer and Godly counsel. Shield him from evil. Establish his trust again and again in YOU ALONE. Pour out YOUR LOVE into _____ heart and let it run into the dry places, refreshing him, empowering him as YOUR Leader.
YOUR WORD says, *"When men are brought low, LIFT THEM UP." Job 22:29a*
In Jesus' Name, I pray.

"They shall LIFT UP their voice, they shall sing for the majesty of the Lord." Isaiah 2:14

Majestic Lord sing through _____ with power and grace, grace which he will obtain in his sanctuary and power because a clean heart filled with YOUR SPIRIT is power! Come Lord Jesus, bring our people into YOUR PRESENCE with hearts prepared to love. Sing over us. Awaken _____ to a song from YOU. In Jesus' Name, I pray.

PRAYER FOR A FAMILY IN SUICIDE RECOVERY

Oh God our God;
I cannot fathom a young woman so unhappy, so isolated as to end her life.
YOU are the Comforter and the only one for her parents to turn to now.
Protect their minds from desperation. Somehow reach down into their
hearts and begin to reveal YOUR LOVE. There will never be answers to
satisfy their questions. They must find a way to live. Bring support to them
from others and help them receive. For the remainder of their earthy lives,
may they find YOU are there, moment to moment, year after year.
ALL SUFFICIENT ONE carry this deep hurt. Comfort them. Cause them
to seek after YOUR WAYS. YOU ARE ABLE. In Jesus' Name, I pray.

*"I, even I, am he that comforteth you: who art thou, that thou shouldest be afraid
of a man that shall die, and of the son of man which shall be made as grass"*
Isaiah 51:12

PRAYER FOR A RUNAWAY

Loving Counselor;
We come after _____ today in prayer.
Praise YOU for godly grandparents who will not let go in prayer!
Lord, wherever she is – provide safety, food, clothing and shelter but we
ask in Jesus' Name that she come to the end of herself.
Let no drug or alcohol satisfy.
We ask that she CANNOT PARTAKE of them. We pray that no
enticement will work. Shut down all relationships feeding this rebellion
Speak to her parents in clear and definite terms.
YOU are the Sovereign Lord.
YOU will not be mocked.
YOU care for YOUR own.
YOU allow consequences brought on by choice BUT YOU restore and
deliver.
Holy Spirit, run after this young woman today and hedge her in from
destruction. Bring her back to Truth, we pray. Waking or sleeping, draw
her to YOU through dreams, visions, scripture, music, people, and places.
Bring her home.
Praise YOU that YOU hear our cry!
YOU have set apart the godly for YOUR purposes and when we call, YOU
will answer.
We are calling out today for _____ in love and expectancy because

YOU CARE, Mighty Burden Bearer, we present her to YOU in prayer. Bless her and rescue her from herself. In Jesus' Name, I pray.

"But know that the LORD hath set apart him that is godly for himself: the LORD will hear when I call unto him."
Psalm 4:3

MY PRAYER FOR THIS BOOK

Spirit of the Living God, fall fresh on me.
Cleanse me.
Mold me.
Break me.
Fill me.
Pour out YOUR Heart Love for others into mine.
Birth the beauty, challenge and reward found in praying for others.
Show me how to tap this amazing source long neglected by the church and rarely found in the world.
It is the work left to do.
YOU have willingly given it to us.
YOU have placed this burden upon me.
By YOUR GRACE this book will come to be.

Stir up the truth of Your Word within me.
Urge me to write, proclaim and pray through
Releasing hope through the stories of others who believe and testify to prayer.
Galvanize YOUR people all over the world to pray.
Encounter us so we may surge in prayer and become a praying people.

Today I need a window of assurance and light breaking through; the autumn rain to grow my faith for the journey toward godliness must constantly embrace praying for others.
Cause the outline, scriptures, references and the lens of experience to flow together.
Teach me.
Train me.
Take my hand Precious Lord, lead me.
In Jesus' Name, I pray.

Lord Jesus, Intercessor,
Creator of the sea
Teach us the tide's great secret
Of quiet urgency.
Spindrift of words we ask not,
But Lord, we seek to know
The conquering patience of the tides,
Whatever winds may blow

Amy Carmichael

A COMPASSIONATE DETERMINATION

Every morning lean thine arms awhile
Upon the window sill of heaven
And gaze upon thy Lord.
Then, with vision in thy heart,
Turn to meet thy day.

Thomas Blake

ABOUT THE AUTHOR

Billie Cash is an international retreat and conference speaker/musician. She has authored three other books, *Windows of Assurance, Light Breaking Through* and *Autumn Rain*. With humor and insight, she brings accountability. A fresh authenticity and personal application are the keys to her ministry.

Billie Cash
1605 N. Germantown Pkwy; Suite 111
Cordova, TN 38018
Website: www.billiecash.com
E-Mail: brcash@midsouth.rr.com

I would love to hear from you!

INDEX OF BIBLE TRANSLATIONS

All scripture used is from the New International Version unless otherwise indicated. Other translations used:

CEV Contemporary English Version
Grand Rapids: Zondervan (1965)

KJV King James Version
New York: American Bible Society (1611)

LB Living Bible
Wheaton: Tyndale House (1979)

Msg The Message
Colorado Springs: Navpress (1993)

NASB New American Standard
Anaheim: Foundation Press (1978)

NIV New International Version
Garden City: Doubleday (1985)

NLT New Living Translation
Wheaton: Tyndale House (1996)

PRAYERSURGE NOTES

CHAPTER I

1. Quoted from *Storm Surge*, p.1 http://hurricanes.noaa. gov/prepare/surge.htm
2. Merton: *Thomas Merton* edited by *Jonathan Montaldo, Dialogues With Silence* (San Francisco: Harper, 2001), 57
3. 2 Timothy 2:19

CHAPTER 2

1. Matthew 6:5
2. Matthew 6:6
3. Matthew 6:9
4. Luke 11:9
5. Luke 18:1
6. I Samuel 1:3
7. I Samuel 1:11
8. I Samuel 1:13
9. I Samuel 1:15-16
10. I Samuel 1:17
11. I Samuel 1:20b
12. I Samuel 2: 1, 2, 3, 7, 8b, 9, 10
13. I Samuel 3:9b
14. 1 Samuel 3:21
15. *Louf: Andre Louf* edited by *Richard J. Foster* and *Emilie Griffin*, Spiritual Classics (San Francisco: Harper, 2000,33
16. Karon: Jan Karon, Shepherds Abiding (New

York: Penguin, 2003), 111

CHAPTER THREE.

1. Whitney: Donald Whitney, Spiritual Disciplines for the Christian Life (Colorado: Navpress, 1991), 70
2. Steer: Roger Steer, Spiritual Secrets of George Muller (Wheaton: Shaw, 1985), 60-62
3. Psalms 139: 1-4
4. Ibid, v 5
5. Ibid, v13
6. Ibid, vv 17-18
7. Ibid, vv 23-24
8. James 5:16

CHAPTER FOUR

1. Ephesians 3:14-16
2. James 4:8
3. Dailey: Jerome Dailey, Soul Space (Brentwood: Integrity, 2003), 23.
4. Psalm 1:6
5. I Thessalonians 5:8
6. Philippians 4:5
7. Matthew 14:31-32
8. John 18: 17
9. Lewis: C. S. Lewis, The Screwtape Letters (San Francisco: Harper, 1996), 38.
10. Ortburg: John Ortburg, If You

Want To Walk On Water,
You've Got To Get Out Of
The Boat (Grand Rapids:
Zondervan, 2001), 23.

11. Hebrews 12: 7a, 12,13a

12. Ortburg: John Ortburg, If You
Want To Walk On Water,
You've Got To Get Out Of
The Boat (Grand Rapids:
Zondervan, 2001), 24.

13. John 21:15a

14. Hebrews 6:10

CHAPTER FIVE

1. Hebrews 6:19a

2. Philippians 4:6

3. Acts 1:14 NLT

4. Murray: Andrew Murray,
The Secret of Intercession
(New Kensington: Whitaker
House, 1995), 7

5. Quoted from article,
Andrew Murray by David
Smithers p.1,
www.watchword.org/smithers/
andrewmurray

6. Murray: Andrew Murray,
The Secret Of Intercession
(New Kensington: Whitaker
House, 1995), 99.

7. Du Plessis: J. Du Plessis,
The Life of Andrew Murray
of South Africa (Marshall
Morgan and Scott, 1919) p,
460f

8. Daniel 1:4-5

9. Daniel 1:15a, 17

10. Daniel 6:4

11. Daniel 6:7b

12. Daniel 6:10

13. Daniel 6:16b

14. Daniel 6:20-21

15. Daniel 6:23

16. Daniel 6:26-27

17. I Peter 1:7

18. Carmichael: Amy
Carmichael, The Edges of
His Ways (Fort Washington:
Christian Literature
Crusade, 1998) p77.

CHAPTER SIX

1. Philippians 1:9

2. Proverbs 10:5

3. Cymbala: Jim Cymbala,
God's Grace From Ground
Zero (Grand Rapids:
Zondervan, 2001) p10-11

4. Ibid, p12

5. http://www.legacy.com/
LegacyTribute/Sept11.asp?P
age+TributeStory&PersonId
+113373

6. Galatians 6:2

7. http://cnn.com/
specials/2004/tsunami.
disaster,
http://cnn.com/2005/
worldasia.pcf/12/
27quakefacts

8. Revelation 15:4

9. http://cnn.com Survivor's
tale: This is Surreal by Alan
Morison- Jan 24, 2005

10. I Peter 5:7 TLB

CHAPTER SEVEN

1. Isaiah 57:14-15 The
Message

2. Kidd: Sue Monk Kidd, The
   Secret Life of Bees (New
   York: Penguin Putnam,
   2002) p.147
3. Jude 1:20-21
4. Romans 8:14 The Message
5. Romans 8:26 The Message
6. Jude 1:22b
7. John 14:13a
8. Psalm 112:1
9. Psalm 112:2
10. Psalm 112:3
11. Psalm 112:4
12. Psalm 112:5a
13. Psalm 112:5b-9
14. Psalm 116:5-6

CHAPTER EIGHT

1. II Chronicles 16:9
2. Psalm 40:8
3. I Kings 8:43, I Chronicles
   28:9, Isaiah 43:10
4. Isaiah 53:10
5. I Thessalonians 5:17-18
6. Philippians 2:13
7. Hurnard: Hannah Hurnard,
   Watchmen on the Wall
   (Nashville: Broadman
   Holman, 1997) p.68

CHAPTER NINE

1. Fosdick: Harry Emerson
   Fosdick, The Meaning Of
   Prayer (London: YMCA,
   1915) p.161
2. Isaiah 41:10
3. Hebrews 3:8
4. I John 1:9
5. I Samuel 16:7b

6. Psalm 51:10.
7. Nouwen: Henri Nowen,
   The Only Necessary Thing
   (New York: Crossroad,
   1999) pp 198-199
8. Stephens, Gray: Dr. Steve
   Stephens and Alice Gray,
   The Worn Out Woman
   (Sisters: Multnomah, 2004)
   p.17
9. II Corinthians 10:4-5
   NEB
10. Elliot: Elisabeth Elliot, Keep
    A Quiet Heart (Ann Arbor:
    Vine, 1995) p110
11. I Peter 5:8
12. Ephesians 6:12
13. Matthew 4:3
14. James 4:7
15. Proverbs 15:8b
16. Piper: John Piper, The
    Pleasures of God (Sisters:
    Multonmah 1991) p215
17. I Peter 3:12
18. Graham: Ruth Bell Graham
    Legacy of A Pack Rat
    (Nashville: Thomas Nelson,
    1989) p.53
19. Psalm 100:2,3a, 4
20. Carmichael: Amy
    Carmichael, Edges of His
    Ways (Fort Washington:
    Christian Literature
    Crusade, 1998) p.92
21. Isaiah 65:24

CHAPTER TEN

1. Smith: Gordon Smith, On

The Way (Colorado Springs: Navpress, 2001) p.71
2. Ibid.
3. Mark 1:35
4. Matthew 12:30
5. Acts 4:13b
6. Acts 4:20
7. Acts 4:24a, 29
8. Warren: Rick Warren, Better Together (Lake Forest: Purpose Driven, 2004) p160.
9. Acts 1:14 NLT
10. Cash: Carey H. Cash, A Table In The Presence (Nashville; W Publishing, 2004) p90
11. Ibid p.164
12. Leiner: Kathereine Leiner, Digging Out (New York: NAL, 2004) p.156
13. Ecclesiastes 3:1,5

CHAPTER ELEVEN

1. Isaiah 59:15-16 NASB
2. Isaiah 59:16 AMP
3. Isaiah 59:16b CEV
4. Isaiah 59:16 The Message
5. Psalm 86:11a
6. Prater: Arnold Prather, You Can Pray As You Ought (Nashville: Thomas Nelson, 1977) p 61.
7. I Corinthians 11:24
8. Prater: Arnold Prather, You Can Pray As You Ought (Nashville: Thomas Nelson, 1977) p.62 and 64
9. Luke 18:4-5
10. Luke 18:7-8
11. Exodus 32:9
12. Exodus 32:11
13. Exodus 32:14
14. Esther 2:2
15. Esther 1:12a
16. Esther 2:7
17. Esther 2:11
18. Esther 2:12
19. Matthew 6:18b
20. Esther 4:16
21. Jones: Timothy Jones, The Art Of Prayer, (Colorado Springs: Waterbrook 2005) p91-92

CHAPTER TWELVE

1. Psalm 96:3
2. Isaiah 61:3b
3. Psalm 4:3
4. Piper: John Piper, The Pleasures of God, (Sisters: Multnomah, 2000) p227
5. Ephesians 6:19
6. Colossians 4:3
7. II Thessalonians 3:1
8. Bingham: Derek Bingham, A Shiver of Wonder, (Belfast: Ambassador Intl, 2004) p.216
9. Jeremiah 46:7
10. Bingham: Derek Bingham, The Wild-Bird Child, (Belfast: Ambassador Intl, 2003) p19-20.
11. Psalm 27:8

OTHER BOOKS BY AUTHOR

WINDOWS OF ASSURANCE

In her Journey of Prayer, Billie Cash shares the resources she used to persevere as a school girl in 33 different schools. Those experiences propelled Billie into the artificial light of the theater; but it was the penetrating light of God's presence that birthed identity and ready resolve. For each window she opened, His love met her with grace and called her to test the real release of prevailing prayer.

ISBN: 1 889893 59 5
$12.99/£8.99 (224 pp)

LIGHT BREAKING THROUGH

Light. The visible reminder of Invisible Light. (T. S. Eliot) The light of God searches all things, our struggles, lonliness and brokenness. This book lets us experience that light, as it breaks through our struggles, intercepting us with truth, love, and fresh insights at every turn, in every season. He urges us onward, to continue, to grow, to believe, to love, and to finish our race, giving us illumination in the darkest days. We can trust His Light.

ISBN: 1 889893 97 8
$9.99/£6.99 (144 pp)

AUTUMN RAIN

This book is a message of faith's journey, having a beginning, becoming dependent, being responsible, fruitful and then transforming the landscape through transplanted lives. The metaphor of the garden is carried throughout the book; beginning faith is nurtured by Spring rain but transforming faith has a harvest, an abundance brought by the autumn rain, the rain of harvest. It is a faith that continues to change the landscape of life.

ISBN: 1 932307 33 8
$11.99/£7.99 (224 pp)